T0038903

THE
ATLAS
OF
CHRISTMAS

THE MERRIEST, TASTIEST, QUIRKIEST
HOLIDAY TRADITIONS
FROM AROUND THE WORLD

ALEX PALMER

RUNNING PRESS
PHILADELPHIA

Running Press
Hachette Book Group
1290 Avenue of the Americas, New York, NY 10104
www.runningpress.com
@Running_Press

Printed in China
First Edition: October 2020

Published by Running Press, an imprint of Perseus Books, LLC, a subsidiary
of Hachette Book Group, Inc. The Running Press name and logo is a trademark
of the Hachette Book Group.

The Hachette Speakers Bureau provides a wide range of authors
for speaking events. To find out more, go to
www.hachettespeakersbureau.com or call (866) 376-6591.

The publisher is not responsible for websites
(or their content) that are not owned by the publisher.

Print book cover and interior design by Amanda Richmond.

Library of Congress Control Number:2020936262

ISBNs: 978-0-7624-7039-6 (hardcover), 978-0-7624-7040-2 (ebook)

1010

10 9 8 7 6 5 4 3

CONTENTS

7. FIERCE COMPETITIONS AND LEISURELY PASTIMES

☆
INTRODUCTION

*I*f you picked up this book, there is probably something you love about Christmas: a certain song that gets played every year, a special cookie your grandmother baked during the season, or just the simple scent of evergreen that fills the stores and city streets. Whatever your age, interests, or religious affiliation, there is some Christmas tradition that appeals to you. It's a holiday that offers something for everyone—even self-proclaimed Scrooges.

That's true throughout the world, too. More than any other holiday, Christmas has been adapted and interpreted by different countries and communities to suit their particular culture. Santa Claus may be the holiday heavyweight in North America, but in many Spanish-speaking countries, kids stay up late waiting for the three Wise Men, while Italians look for a jolly lady riding a broomstick. You might kick off the season by putting up a Christmas tree in your living room, but for others, the must-have decoration might be a goat made of straw, a sparkly spiderweb, or a log with a smiley face that poops candy (see page 80 for more about him).

Christmas celebrations around the world are as distinctive, varied, and surprising as the people themselves. In this book, I've set out to capture this range in all its rich variety and explore how a tradition, whether a colorful ornament or peculiar character, tells a much deeper story about that country or culture. And while *The Atlas of Christmas* is by no means comprehensive, it does aim to offer an entertaining survey of the many ways Christmas is honored the world over—whether extravagant or intimate, sacred or silly.

There are so many reasons to celebrate the Christmas season. So grab a mug of hot chocolate and your favorite Christmas sweater—unless you live in one of the many places where Christmas takes place during the summer, in which case, grab your best Santa sunglasses—and get ready for some festive fun.

Merry Christmas!

Albanian—*Gëzuar Krishtlindjet*

Croatian—*Sretan Bozic*

Danish—*Glædelig jul*

Dutch—*Zalig Kerstfeest*

Estonian—*Rôômsaid Jôule*

Farsi—*Cristmas mobArak*

German—*Frohe Weihnachten*

Greek—*Eftihismena Christougenna*

Hindi—*Shub Naya Baras*

Icelandic—*Gleðileg jól*

Irish—*Nollaig shona dhuit*

Italian—*Buon Natale*

Japanese—*Merii Kurisumasu*

Korean—*Sung Tan Chuk Ha*

Mandarin—*Kung His Hsin Nien bing Chu Shen Tan*

Polish—*Wesolych swiat*

Portuguese—*Boas-festas*

Romanian—*Craciun fericit*

Russian—*Schastlivogo Rozhdestva*

Spanish—*Feliz Navidad*

Vietnamese—*Chuc mung Giang Sinh*

Part One

CELEBRATIONS
AROUND
THE WORLD

Chapter One

CEREMONIES

and

RITUALS

While Christmas began as a day to honor
the birth of Jesus, just how this is done has grown
and evolved in some surprising ways throughout
the world. The approaches that different countries
take to recognizing the season reflect their particular
history and heritage, and how cultures adapt
the same materials to suit their own place.

LAS POSADAS: FESTIVAL OF ACCEPTANCE

MEXICO

*T*he story of Christ's birth remains the central focus of Christmas celebrations throughout Latin America and Spanish-speaking parts of the world. But while nativity scenes and tributes to the Virgin Mary and Wise Men are widespread, the people of Mexico take a slightly different path in honoring the tale. A man and woman dress up as Joseph and Mary and reenact the search for lodging on the night when Jesus was born. The couple, often played by adolescents, leads a procession of children costumed in silver and gold robes as well as musicians and other parishioners to a pre-designated house. This is the *posada*, or inn, and the residents take on the role of skeptical innkeepers of Bethlehem. They greet the visitors at the door, listen as the couple explains their plight, and reluctantly refuse them entry. But after some further back-and-forth, typically in song or verse, the innkeepers finally recognize the holy couple and warmly allow them inside.

The whole procession moves indoors, where participants gather around the nativity scene to pray, read scripture, and sing carols before moving on to the next *posada*—often visiting three or four homes in a night. From the last *posada*, everyone heads to Mass, after which they cut loose with a more relaxed party that usually includes feasting on tamales, *pan dulce*, and *champurrado* (a corn-based hot chocolate popular in Mexico) while the children take shots at a clay piñata full of candy and fruit.

While some celebrate *las posadas* only on Christmas Eve, many perform the ritual every night from December 16 to December 24—nine nights, representing the nine months of Mary's pregnancy. The specific songs may vary and for some performances, Joseph and Mary may even ride atop donkeys or incorporate other dramatic elements. The tradition dates back to at least the seventeenth century, introduced by Augustinian missionaries as a Christian alternative to the Aztec custom of celebrating the god Huitzilopochtli at about the same time of year. The practice grew more popular over time and spread throughout Latin America. The performance of requesting and being granted shelter—after several denials—has particular resonance for Mexican American immigrant communities of the United States.

Mexico is not the only country where you might find such reenactments of Joseph and Mary's search for lodging. Parts of Austria and Germany also still see performances of *Herbergsuchen* ("Search for the Inn"). They are in some ways a remnant of the nativity and mystery plays that were popular throughout medieval Europe, which portrayed the birth of Jesus and events surrounding it and which largely died out after the Protestant Reformation.

THREE KINGS DAY:
THREE CHEERS FOR THE MAGI

SPAIN AND LATIN AMERICA

*W*hile the Holy Family is the center of any nativity scene, another trio gets their day a little later in the Christmas season. For Christians in many countries, the official end to the Christmas season is January 6, the twelfth day of Christmas, known as Epiphany. This day recognizes the tale of the three Wise Men, collectively known as the Magi, arriving in Bethlehem to pay tribute to baby Jesus with gifts of gold, frankincense, and myrrh. Upon seeing him, they had the epiphany that he was indeed the son of God.

The event is celebrated in different ways throughout the world (see box) but one of the most prevalent celebrations is *el Día de los Tres Reyes Magos*, or Three Kings Day, in Spain and Latin American countries. This is often a bigger day of feasting and gift giving than Christmas itself (which tends to be more focused on attending Mass and church services). The evening before, children will write letters to the Magi and leave their shoes out at night—usually with some hay to feed the Wise Men's hungry camels—in hopes they will be filled with treats the next day. On the day of Epiphany itself, extravagant parades accompany the Magi as they roll via camel, boat, or even helicopter, grabbing letters written by children in the streets and bringing gifts with them to pass along to the kids.

Wherever it's celebrated, the party always includes some kind of showstopping cake, from the fruit-bejeweled *roscón de reyes* in Spain to the flaky *galette des rois* frangipane-filled pastry of Belgium. The forms and flavors of "king cake" vary significantly, but all include some kind of hidden prize—an almond, dried bean, or ceramic baby—that when found earns the recipient the honor of "king for a day" or some other similar distinction. (For more about king cake, see page 208.)

A few other very distinctive ways that Epiphany is celebrated throughout the world:

BLESSING OF THE WATER

In countries where the Eastern Orthodox Church is prevalent, such as Russia, Greece, and Bulgaria, Epiphany is celebrated with a blessing of a large body of water –followed by a dip into it. Taking place on January 19 (following the Julian calendar), this usually involves a visit to a wintry lake or ocean, and in chillier areas, even cutting holes in the ice to access the frigid water below (in some communities, the hole cut into the ice might be in the shape of a cross). A priest or bishop may toss a cross into the water or say a prayer and the participants take a deep breath and jump in, sometimes dunking their heads three times, representing the holy trinity.

MAGI'S BLESSING

In German-speaking countries, children known as *Sternsinger* ("star singers") will go from house to house singing an Epiphany carol, urging the Magi to bless each home. They'll then chalk the initials of the Magi onto the door, usually incorporating the year as well, creating something like this (for the year 2020): 20 ✝ C ✝ M ✝ B ✝ 20. Not only do the letters reference the Wise Men, Caspar, Melchior, and Balthasar, but they also serve as an abbreviation of the Latin phrase *Christus mansionem benedicat*, or "May Christ bless this house."

TWELFTH NIGHT

In Western Christian tradition, Christmas Eve is considered the first night of Christmas, which makes January 5, the eve of Epiphany, the Twelfth Night. And England has long celebrated the holiday enthusiastically—with feasting and singing since at least the medieval era, and later by getting drunk on wassail (a kind of hot mulled cider) and then going wassailing (a kind of door-to-door drunken singing), though that custom has mellowed a bit since its rambunctious heights in the nineteenth century. Today, however, most know "Twelfth Night" as the name of a Shakespeare comedy and from the song "The Twelve Days of Christmas."

WOMEN'S CHRISTMAS

In Ireland, it's celebrated as Nollaig na mBan or "Women's Christmas," as the women of a family, who in more traditional homes have worked so hard preparing feasts throughout the holidays, get a chance to cut loose. The men are expected to handle household duties, including helping to remove the Christmas tree and its decorations, while the ladies gather together with friends or female family members at a home, restaurant, or pub, and even receive gifts from children or other family members.

SINTERKLAAS FESTIVAL:
THE ORIGINAL HOLIDAY OF GIFT GIVING

NETHERLANDS AND BELGIUM

*W*hile the big day of gift giving for much of Latin America falls on Epiphany, for many Europeans, it's one month earlier, during the celebration of a different religious figure. Saint Nicholas of Myra was venerated for centuries for his generosity, and reputed to leave surprise gifts for the youth (read more about him in chapter 4, on page 94). The day in his honor is recognized throughout mainland Europe on December 6—or December 16 for those following the Gregorian calendar. Few places celebrate the figure who would become known as Sinterklaas with more gusto than the Netherlands and Belgium.

Over time, the celebration shifted from a religious and public one where those in need were treated to a feast, to a more private, family-focused, increasingly secular affair. As the celebration has evolved, so has its namesake. While the name of the American Santa Claus is a corruption of Sinterklaas and the two characters now share a number of traits (red-and-white wardrobes, white beards, and a habit of popping down chimneys to deliver gifts), the two figures are distinct. In Dutch, Santa is known as *de Kerstman* or "the Christmas man," and he is a secondary figure compared to his forebear. It is certainly tough to compete with Sinterklaas's theatrical flair.

In the Netherlands and Belgium today, festivities officially begin on the first Saturday following November 11. Sinterklaas arrives "from Spain" by steamboat into the designated seaside town (which varies from one year to the next in Holland, and is always Antwerp in Belgium). His assistant, Zwarte Piet (see page 130 for more on him), tosses sweets to the waiting crowd. Sinterklaas then disembarks, hops onto a white horse, and parades through the street. Over the following days, other towns will have their own Sinterklaas arrival celebrations, and the gift bringer will pop into schools, hospitals, and community gathering areas—all leading up to Saint Nicholas's Day.

On the night before the big day, the character is said to travel from rooftop to rooftop on his horse (no sleigh or reindeer for this guy), leaving gifts, chocolate coins, or other sweets in the shoes of the boys and girls who have left their footwear by the fireplace, usually with a carrot or some hay and water for Sinterklaas's horse to munch on (though naughty children might get a switch or a stick for bad behavior). The good bishop might leave a note or poem, and sometimes wraps the gift in an elaborate style known as a *surprise* (see page 165).

In much of the Netherlands, Saint Nicholas's Day is the predominant gift-giving occasion, with more than half the Dutch people exchanging gifts on December 6, and 36 percent doing so only that day and not on Christmas. But in Belgium and Southern Netherlands, it's an occasion set aside for children, and adults will exchange gifts later in the month, on Christmas.

Parts of Germany also celebrate Saint Nicholas's Day with fervor. The bishop will appear on horseback and may ask how children have behaved that year or quiz them on church doctrine and request that they sing a hymn, in exchange for a gift, of course. Instead of Zwarte Piet, in Germany he's likely accompanied by a more sinister sidekick, such as Knecht Ruprecht or Krampus (read more about them in chapter 5, "Devils and Troublemakers").

WEIHNACHTSMÄRKTE: THE BUSTLING BIRTHPLACE OF MODERN CHRISTMAS

GERMANY

*G*ermany has been celebrating Christmas going back to at least the eighth century, when Winfrid, Saint Boniface, introduced the Germanic tribes to Christianity. And it has brought the world a number of Christmas customs that have been widely adopted, including Christmas trees, Christmas ornaments, Advent calendars, and Advent wreaths, to name a few. But few practices embody Germany's influence on how we now celebrate the holiday more than the *Weihnachtsmärkte*—Christmas markets.

Seemingly every German town square is taken over by buzzing booths selling baked goods, Christmas decorations, handmade wooden toys, and all manner of other merchandise ideal for celebrating the holidays. Brass bands play while visitors sip on cups of glühwein or snack on gingerbread hearts as they view the goods on offer, stopping by the nativity scene (featuring either wooden figures or real people) reliably set in the center of the market.

Today, such activity might not sound all that remarkable; such Christmas markets can be found in practically every Western city of more than a few dozen people. But none of these places, however charming they may be, exude the history and legacy of the *Weihnachtsmärkte*. From at least as far back as the fourteenth century until as late as the mid-twentieth century, these were the primary places for locals to pick up their Christmas decorations. During the eighteenth and nineteenth centuries, travelers from around the world would visit Germany and, struck by the geniality and kindness on display, even in a place of public commerce, return with sentimental descriptions of the holiday magic they'd seen. These impressions would shape how the rest of the Western world practiced Christmas.

As other markets and street fairs died away in the face of industrialization and mass production, the Christmas market persisted. While the oldest still-operating market is in Munich (where it has been in operation for about six hundred years), the largest and most famous is Nuremberg's Christkindlesmarkt. In the shadow of the sixty-foot-tall Schöner Brunnen ("Beautiful Fountain") and six-century old *Frauenkirche* ("Church of Our Lady"), more than one hundred booths offer up gifts and treats. The name of the market, which has been in operation since 1697, translates to Christ Child Market, in reference to the angelic gift-bringing figure of the Christkindl (see page 103), who appears each year during the market's opening day at the top of the church before descending to greet the thousands of visitors who are there ready to shop.

Travelers can now arrange for weeklong "Christmas market tours" and Germany boasts more than two thousand *Weihnachtsmärkte* sprinkled across the country.

Advent calendars are among Germany's many Christmas inventions that have been part of the holiday for centuries. Advent is the period that begins the fourth Sunday before Christmas Day and is celebrated each Sunday leading up to it by faiths including Roman Catholic, Lutheran, Anglican and Episcopal Churches. Advent calendars were first introduced by Lutherans in the mid-nineteenth century to help children count off the days leading up to Christmas. At first handmade, they began to be sold by printing companies beginning around 1903 and after World War II, Stuttgart printer Richard Sellmer Verlag began mass-producing them, introducing the first Advent calendar to the U.S. in the late 1940s. These early versions often included a Bible verse for each day, before chocolates and all variety of other treats became the norm.

Prince Albert, husband of Queen Victoria, is credited with introducing the English-speaking world to a number of his native Germany's holiday practices. While it's an exaggeration to say he's the main reason that England began putting up Christmas trees, he did help spread the idealized image of a family Christmas, with tables stacked high with gifts and goodies and decorations everywhere. The widely circulated illustrations of Victoria and Albert's Christmas ignited the imaginations of those who aspired to create a royal domestic bliss. Many of the older, more raucous English traditions, such as mumming and wassail-fueled festivities, had gone out of fashion and the public was eager for a more modern way to celebrate. It turned out Germany, and their German-born monarch, offered just what they were seeking.

SAINT LUCIA PROCESSIONS: PARADE OF WHITE

SWEDEN

*N*icholas is not the only saint to be celebrated during the Christmas season. On December 13, the feast day of Saint Lucia is recognized as an opportunity to honor Lucia of Syracuse, who was martyred during persecutions of Christians in the early fourth century. While she's a venerated figure in the Roman Catholic Church, in Sweden, the celebration of Saint Lucia has little to do with that story, beyond the fact that the Italian folk song "Santa Lucia" can usually be heard during the various gatherings. Just as jolly old Saint Nick bears only the slightest resemblance to Saint Nicholas of Myra, Sweden's Saint Lucia is a gift-bearing character with little similarity to her Catholic namesake. Portrayed as a young blond (it is Sweden, after all) girl dressed in white with a red sash and crown of lingonberry sprigs, she is meant to symbolize innocence and light in the midst of midwinter darkness—especially important in a place where the night can stretch as long as eighteen hours.

On Saint Lucia's Day, kids dressed in long white gowns parade through shopping malls, government buildings, and nearly every other place where people gather. In each parade, one girl represents Sankta Lucia, leading the procession wearing her Advent wreath crown, complete with glowing candles (usually electric ones these days), followed by a number of *stjärngossar* ("star boys") wearing cone-shaped hats made of silver paper and decorated with stars.

Every city crowns its own Lucia "Queen of Light," all the way up to a national Lucia, crowned in Stockholm. Thanks to some miraculously good timing, Saint Lucia's Day falls just three days after the Nobel Prize award ceremony, held each year on December 10 in Sweden's capital. Since many of the winners remain in the city for various events, the national procession has for years begun the day with "wake-up calls" for the Nobel laureates staying at Stockholm's Grand Hôtel. Beginning at about 7 a.m., the procession of white-clad kids (who have been given the laureates' room keys, with their permission) make their way from room to room, singing the scientists, academics, and authors awake like some kind of angelic Christmas alarm clock.

While many cultures celebrate the Twelve Days of Christmas, Sweden celebrates Twenty Days of Christmas—from December 26 to January 13, Saint Knut's Day. The closing day of the Swedish holiday season is treated as a party for children, in which decorations are taken down, the Christmas tree is lit one last time before being "plundered" of its ornaments and sweets, and there are plenty of games and singing.

Though celebrated in Sweden, the day is named after Danish king Canute IV, who was assassinated by his cousin and rival in the eleventh century, sparking a civil war. It may end with "throwing out" the Christmas tree, which in previous decades could literally mean tossing the tree out the window but now is more likely to mean it's picked up by local volunteer organizations or chopped up and used as firewood. In some regions, the trees are burned in a bonfire.

BURNING THE DEVIL: CLEANSING EVIL SPIRITS BY BONFIRE

GUATEMALA

*T*he holiday season is not only about celebrating peace and goodwill. Just as often, it is a time to symbolically recognize, and exorcise, the darker forces of the world. Like much of Central America, Guatemala is predominantly Roman Catholic and the Christmas season there is focused on the veneration of the Holy Family. But this country also makes time for an incendiary exercise each year meant to burn away bad spirits. On the evening of December 7, at exactly 6 p.m., locals take part in La Quema del Diablo—the "Burning of the Devil" (sometimes called La Quema del Mal Humor). Guatemalans clear out trash from their homes, piling it in the front yard or some other designated area, and then set it on fire. It is viewed as a way to purify the house, while also preparing it for the next day's Feast of the Immaculate Conception, in honor of the Virgin Mary.

Lately, the trash burning has come under fire, so to speak, because so much modern trash consists of plastic and rubber, with mattresses, tires, and more ending up in the pyres, releasing toxic chemicals into the air and darkening the clear sky. When approximately half a million fires are being lit in Guatemala City alone, it can cause some serious air quality issues.

There has been some success in encouraging Guatemalans to

stick with burning old newspapers or wood. Instead of approaching the tradition as a literal house cleaning, Guatemalans are urged to view it as a more spiritual cleansing, tossing into the flames papier-mâché effigies of the devil rather than their household garbage. In the Guatemalan city of Antigua, local artists make a human-size devil figure every year, and the whole town comes together to watch it burn. This can create controversy of its own: In 2016, the (topless female) devil that was created was arrested for indecency, and community leaders had to put a corset on the figure to get police to release it in time for the ceremony. Despite the controversies, it's clear that Guatemalans will be burning bad stuff in some form for many years to come.

Burning the Devil is not the only blazing tradition to take place around the Christmas season. Burning effigies is a surprisingly popular holiday pastime around the world.

_____⚪_____

NOCTURNAL PROCESSION OF THE NDOCCIATA
In the southern Italian city of Agnone, this consists of a procession of men, costumed in traditional dress, carry huge fanlike torches through the city streets. Upon arriving to the town square, they ignite a giant "Bonfire of the Brotherhood," meant to burn away negative elements from the past year.

THE BURNING OF THE OLD YEARS

In Ecuador and Honduras, to celebrate the New Year, the locals engage in La Quema de los Años Viejos, or the "Burning of the Old Years," in which they toss effigies of politicians, athletes, or other cultural figures or undesirable objects onto a bonfire. It's meant as a cleansing act and a way to leave behind unpleasantness from the previous year. The effigy masks are often bought separate from the sawdust-stuffed doll bodies and can be customized as preferred.

HOGMANAY

Scotland welcomes in the new year with Hogmanay, which kicks off at midnight on December 31 with fireworks displays, torchlit festivals, and singalongs to Robert Burns's "Auld Lang Syne." The small fishing village of Stonehaven, south of Aberdeen, has developed a particularly incandescent way of celebrating: Locals attach wire cages stuffed with rags and paper to long poles, light them on fire, and march through High Street swinging their homemade fireballs, hurling them into the harbor as the parade concludes.

UP HELLY AA

Stonehaven is not the only flame-happy Scottish festival. In the Shetland Islands, the locals mark the end of winter holidays on the last Tuesday of every January by donning Viking garb, grabbing up torches, and marching through the city streets. The hundreds of costumed men gather around a full-size replica of a Viking longship and toss their lit torches into it, providing a burial ceremony to the previous year while creating a bonfire warm enough to heat the whole city.

TA CHIU FESTIVAL

During Hong Kong's Ta Chiu festival of peace on December 27—primarily a Taoist festival, but one in which local Christians pay tribute to their saints—the names of all local villagers are read from a list, which is then placed on a paper horse and ignited. This fire isn't meant to burn away evil, however, but is believed to send the names up to heaven.

BURNING BROOMS

In the Spanish town of Jarandilla de la Vera, the citizens celebrate the Feast of the Immaculate Conception by igniting brooms, parading them through town and even dueling one another in mock battles before tossing their flaming weapons into a huge bonfire.

YULE LOG NIGHT:
ROLLING UP THE YEAR'S BAD LUCK

LATVIA

*M*any of the most enduring Christmas traditions grew from adapting existing pagan rituals, reframing them with Christian concepts and practices. The Bible did not set down a date for Christ's birth, but pagan Roman festivals such as Saturnalia and Kalends of January were already being celebrated around December 25. Evergreen trees had long decorated homes for year-end festivities (due to their seemingly magical fortitude against cold weather) before they became central to Christmas. And Yule log traditions began in similar ways. By the thirteenth century, the only European region that Christianity hadn't conquered was the Baltics, including what is now the country of Latvia. Pagan traditions survived much longer there than int other places, and accordingly, many pre-Christian rituals have held on, including the Christmastime rolling of the log. Many European cultures burn a Yule log at Christmas, but that's only the last stage of the Latvian Yule Log Night tradition.

After a tree, usually an oak, has been cut down to serve as the family's Yule log, the trunk, or a section of the trunk, is bound with ropes so it can be dragged around town. Members of the village's households don costumes and proceed through the village, dropping in on friends and neighbors for singing and dancing, all while dragging the log along with them. Everywhere the log goes, it is believed to soak up all the misfortune, bad thoughts, and negativity of the old year. After the end of the day's festivities, it's finally brought home to toss into the fireplace or taken to the bonfire and burned. The burning represents the sun regaining its warmth as well as the burning off of all the bad things from the previous year, ensuring the people of the family or town will have a fresh start for the New Year.

For a region that resisted Christianity for so long, Latvia now revels in the holiday's trappings, with Advent calendars, Christmas trees, and gifts proliferating throughout houses. Today, this enthusiasm is compounded by the fact that for decades during Soviet rule, such religious expression was banned. The merry-making around the bonfire now celebrates both the holiday and the freedom to express that joy.

PROCLAMATION OF CHRISTMAS PEACE: PUBLIC CALL FOR ORDER

FINLAND

*C*hristmas is often portrayed as a time when we get past the differences that divided us over the previous year and find some common ground. In Scandinavia, this has become a formal part of the holiday. Known as *joulurauha* in Finnish and *julfrid* in Swedish, the Christmas Peace is a part of Scandinavian tradition that dates back to at least the 1320s. Back then, it was essentially an announcement that anyone who committed a crime on Christmas would get a harsher sentence than usual—an attempt to encourage peace in the public square in the midst of the inevitable holiday rowdiness. Over time, the emphasis shifted to an exhortation that citizens be peaceful and loving to one another during Christmastime.

Several Finnish cities play host to the delaration of Christmas Peace, but the largest celebration takes place in Turku, on the country's southwestern coast, the historical capital of Finland until 1812. At noon on Christmas Eve, a crowd gathers in the Old Great Square, in front of the historic Brinkkala Mansion, singing the hymn "A Mighty Fortress Is Our God." A city official strides out onto the balcony of the stone building, surrounded by fir trees, then reads the proclamation in both Finnish and Swedish, broadcasting it across the country via television and radio:

"Tomorrow, God willing, is the graceful celebration of the birth of our Lord and Savior; and thus is declared a peaceful Christmastime to all, by advising devotion and to behave otherwise quietly and peacefully, because he who breaks this peace and violates the peace of Christmas by any illegal or improper behavior shall under aggravating circumstances be guilty and punished according to what the law and statutes prescribe for each and every offense separately. Finally, a joyous Christmas feast is wished to all inhabitants of the city."

The very earliest wording has been lost to time, but the version that's read now dates back to 1903. The celebrants then all sing the Finnish national anthem, and the ceremony ends with a brief performance by a local military band, officially kicking off the Christmas season.

According to the city of Turku, the declaration of Christmas peace has taken place uninterrupted except on four occasions:

◆ Between 1712 and 1721, during the Greater Wrath, Russia's invasion and occupation of Finland.

◆ Between 1809 and 1815 (though unconfirmed).

◆ In 1917, when Finland's militia was on strike.

◆ In 1939, due to fears of World War II air raids.

EID IL-BURBABA: CELEBRATING SAINT BARBARA

JORDAN, LEBANON AND SYRIA

*W*hile the people of the Middle East are predominantly Muslim, the Christian populations that do live there celebrate the holiday with reverence, typically with a deeply religious observance on Christmas Day itself. But to kick off the season, on December 4, communities throughout the region, particularly in Jordan, Syria, and Lebanon, honor the Christian martyr Saint Barbara with quite a party.

Locals will feast on *burbara*, a dessert made from boiled wheat grains, mixed with sugar, raisins, cinnamon, nuts, pomegranate seeds, and other sweet stuff.

The dessert does not just taste great; it also serves as a reminder of the day's namesake. Saint Barbara is said to have been imprisoned by her pagan father in the third century for converting to Christianity. She then escaped and was concealed from her father thanks to just-planted wheat grains, which grew up around her and covered her path. Though she was eventually found, the wheat remains an important symbol of both the season and Barbara's plight.

In some versions of Saint Barbara's story, she keeps a branch from a cherry tree in her tower prison. On the day she was eventually killed by her father for refusing to renounce her Christianity, the cherry branch is said to have blossomed. (This is a theme in the region, where legend has it all the world's trees bloomed in winter when the Christ Child was born.)

In addition to eating the wheat-based *burbara*, celebrants may also plant wheat grains, lentils, or some other legume on this day. This kicks off the Christmas decorating for the season, and by the time Christmas arrives, they will have typically grown several inches, and the shoots will be used to decorate their nativity scenes.

This tradition of planting wheat seeds that sprout by Christmas Day or Epiphany can be found outside the Middle East, particularly in Provence, where the grains are placed in three small saucers, representing the Holy Trinity.

Further east, in Iraq, where only a small percentage of citizens celebrate Christmas, though the holiday has been publicly celebrated since 2008. The festivities of Iraqi Christians, primarily members of the Chaldean and Assyrian sects, tend to be deeply religious. On Christmas Eve, families celebrate together in the home or just outside in the courtyard. The children read a version of the nativity story while the adults hold candles. When the reading is finished, a pile of thorns is put together and ignited. As the fire burns through the pile, family members sing psalms. If all the thorns burn from end to end, this is seen as a sign of good fortune, and each family member may take turns jumping over the pile of ashes and making a wish.

The Christmas Day celebration takes place at a local religious service. Another, larger bonfire is lit, and the celebrants again sing songs, led by a bishop, often carrying a representation of the baby Jesus, which he then sets on a scarlet cushion and leads in a procession through the church. At the end of the service, the bishop blesses one of the congregants with the Touch of Peace. That person touches the person next to them to pass the blessing on, and the act is repeated until everyone present has received the blessing.

***

What about the place where Jesus is believed to have been born? The town of Bethlehem, in Palestine's West Bank, draws thousands of Christian worshipers from around the globe, but it is generally a muted gathering compared to the rambunctious celebrations in other parts of the world. On Christmas Eve, a procession led by the Latin Patriarch of Jerusalem travels five miles, through Manger Square, ending at the Church of Saint Catherine, where midnight Mass is conducted. The patriarch crosses to the Church of the Nativity, and descends into the grotto below it, where Christ is believed to have been born. There, as the ceremony is broadcast onto screens throughout Manger Square, he places a life-size statue of baby Jesus in a crib.

Chapter 2

MUSICAL
INTERLUDES

and

INTERLOPERS

Christmas is a time of community and connection, and few things have the power to bring people together better than music. Whether it's a hymn chanted in reverent tones at church or a holiday pop song on the car radio, music is central to celebrating Christmas. And around the world, the many ways that music is incorporated into the holiday are as varied as the world's musical traditions themselves.

PARRANDAS:
A LATE-NIGHT MUSICAL STRIKE

PUERTO RICO

*J*f you've ever thrown a Christmas party, you probably did a lot of careful planning and preparation to make sure everyone had enough food and enjoyed themselves. Puerto Rican *parrandas* need no such planning. During the Christmas season, around 10 p.m., a party may just arrive at a person's house whether they planned it or not. A group of singers sneak up to the porch or front yard, the leader gives the signal, and the group bursts into song, playing instruments such as tambourines, maracas, and guitars and serenading those in the home with traditional Puerto Rican Christmas songs, or *aguinaldos*.

Also known as *asalto navideño* or "Christmas assault," *parrandas* are more fun than caroling but a bit more organized than the drunken wassailing traditions popular in England during the seventeenth and eighteenth centuries—disruptive but welcome. Homeowners who were comfortably tucked into bed will get up, throw on the lights inside and outside the house, and have little choice but to invite the *parranderos* into their home and start serving up food and drinks. (It's usually not a *complete* surprise—the partygoers will often drop hints beforehand to make sure the homeowner is up for a party.) The performance is seen as a distinctly Puerto Rican custom and is warmly received even by the local authorities and neighbors who might otherwise make a noise complaint.

After about an hour, or when the food runs out, the party moves on, usually gathering the homeowners themselves into the throng as they move on to the next house. The group continues to grow as the party carries on into the early morning. If the singers are in good spirits and the *coquito* (Puerto Rico's version of eggnog) is flowing, the Christmas assaults can go until the sun comes up. The festivities will usually climax with a meal of *asopao de pollo*, a Puerto Rican chicken soup, at the home of one of the "assaulted."

CAROLS BY CANDLELIGHT: ENSURING NO ONE SPENDS CHRISTMAS ALONE

AUSTRALIA

*A*s the story goes, one December evening in 1937, a Melbourne radio announcer named Norman Banks was walking home and happened to spot an older woman, seemingly home alone, singing Christmas carols along with the radio, her face lit only by candles. He wondered how many other people were celebrating Christmas alone, so he spent the next year organizing an event, inviting anyone who wanted to sing carols with their fellow Australians to make their way to Alexandra Gardens, a park in the city of Melbourne. Ten thousand people showed up, inaugurating the Carols by Candlelight festival that has continued to draw crowds every year since.

It remained in Alexandra Gardens for the next twenty years, evolving into a high-production Christmas concert with full orchestra and celebrity hosts and singers (and usually an appearance by Santa). Over time it became necessary for the event to move to a larger space, and the open-air Sidney Myer Music Bowl bandshell was built specifically for the annual holiday gathering. Since Christmas arrives in Australia just as summer vacation is getting under way, the warm weather makes it an ideal time for an outdoor show, with attendees usually showing up with their folding chairs and blankets.

Versions of the event have spread throughout the country, with events in Commonwealth Park in Canberra, the Supreme Court Gardens in Perth, and Elder Park in Adelaide. While the performers and songs vary, typically those showing up will be handed song sheets of the carols being sung that night along with a candle (now typically in a protective case). The funds almost always go to charity and tradition dictates that each concert wraps up with everyone joining in a rendition of the hymn "Let There Be Peace on Earth." Although Melbourne hosts the oldest Carols by Candlelight event, Sydney's has grown into the largest, taking place in the city's Domain public park. In 2018, nearly fifty thousand people attended Carols in the Domain. The bigger shows are televised and have become appointment viewing for many Australians. That old woman singing by herself would no doubt feel far from alone today.

JUNKANOO: A CARIBBEAN CHRISTMAS EXTRAVAGANZA

BAHAMAS

$\mathcal{I}$n the Bahamas, as well as other English-speaking Caribbean nations, the Christmas festivities don't end on December 25. The next day—really, a few hours after Christmas Day—is the festival of Junkanoo, a brightly colored parade full of music, dance, and elaborate costumes that resembles Mardi Gras through a Caribbean lens. Starting in the early hours of the morning (the better to avoid the intense Caribbean heat), hundreds of people take to the streets. Musicians play cowbells, brass horns, conch shells, and goatskin drums; dancers perform intricate routines; and elaborately costumed figures in animal masks and huge headdresses stand atop equally elaborate floats. The procession marches down Nassau's main stretch of Bay Street, bringing an explosion of color and energy to the early morning. It wraps up shortly after sunrise with a costume judging and awarding of prizes.

But probably the most astounding thing about Junkanoo is that just days after its celebration on Boxing Day, Bahamians do it all over again, kicking off another over-the-top parade at 1 a.m. on January 1.

The costumes are astonishing—complex detail reaching as high as fifteen feet—made, usually by the wearers themselves, from simple materials like cardboard, wire, and crepe paper, over months. The lightweight materials are essential considering the wearer must be on their feet, dancing, for eight hours or more. The handmade tradition dates back to the origin of Junkanoo more than two centuries ago, when celebrants would incorporate whatever was available—feathers, tissue paper, plants, and even sea sponges—to create inventive outfits.

The celebration comes from the African slaves brought to the islands in the eighteenth century, not only in the Bahamas but in Belize, Jamaica, Guatemala, and even North and South Carolina in the United States. British law dictated that slaves be given three days off for Christmas, likely the only time of the year with that much rest, so it was celebrated with singing, dancing, and mask making. After British slavery was abolished in 1807, the celebration continued and evolved, and has grown more elaborate from one year to the next.

But what about the name? Theories include that it is a reference to the French *gens inconnus* ("unknown people"), since participants wear masks, or that it comes from the English name given to a merchant-turned-warrior based in modern-day Ghana.

The festival has faced its share of setbacks, such as a prohibition on performing on Nassau's Bay Street in place from 1933 to 1947. But Junkanooers found other places to congregate and the ban was eventually lifted. Today, Junkanoo is respected as a national treasure, with costume making taught in workshops and music preserved in recordings. Despite plenty of challenges, the music continues.

COLINDE:
ANCIENT MIDWINTER MELODIES

ROMANIA AND MOLDOVA

*W*hile many yuletide traditions around the world include Christmas carols, the *colinde* of Romania and Moldova are considered the most important tradition of the holidays in those countries. The caroling is older than Christmas itself, dating back to pagan winter solstice rituals and the Roman festival of Saturnalia before being adapted to the Christmas holiday. *Colinde* began as choral songs that male singers would perform, going from farm to farm as part of a ritual requesting the return of the sun.

As Christianity became more widely practiced beginning in the ninth century, the songs were adapted to the Eastern Orthodox faith, with biblical lyrics relating to the nativity and Mary in particular, though they would still incorporate nonbiblical subjects such as popular mythology, marriage, and family. The tradition continues, and the enduring significance of the *colinde* earned it a place on UNESCO's World Heritage list of Intangible Cultural Heritage of Humanity in 2013.

Today, the singing groups, still usually composed only of men, may form weeks in advance, with sometimes daily rehearsals to ensure they are ready to perform on Christmas Eve. The singers go from house to house offering up their songs, sometimes tailoring the lyrics to a specific host. In addition to these deferential pieces, they may also perform more danceable tunes, enticing the unmarried women of the home to join in the celebration. Depending on the region or individual group, they may wear traditional costumes or play flutes and drums. In exchange, the host will usually offer up food and drink to the entertainers.

And as it happens, New Year's gets its own set of carols. They are performed in a ceremony called Plugusorul. The word itself literally means "little plow," and indeed, involves performers ritually plowing and sowing, using a plow decorated with colored paper and embroidered cloth, as they recite songs related to fertility and bountiful crops in the year ahead. In some places, the plow has been replaced by a goat.

While Romania has *colinde*, further south, Greece has its own caroling tradition of *kalanda*. Merrymakers go door to door singing and playing harmonicas, triangles and other simple instruments. But they also carry carved, sometimes illuminated ships known as *karavaki* into which they will toss any coins or sweets they receive for their performances. Decorated model ships are a common sight in households throughout Greece, where the men were often out at sea and the boats became symbols of safe returns. In recent years, cultural and environmental advocates have urged that these ships replace Christmas trees as the main symbol of the holiday in Greece.

ZAMPOGNA:
A CHRISTMAS BAGPIPE

ITALY

*S*cotland does not have a global monopoly on the bagpipe. Italians have their own version of the well-known woodwind, known as a *zampogna*. Like the more familiar instrument, this one also has a large goatskin or sheepskin sack that the player must inflate with air, but the *zampogna* has multiple chanters (playable pipes with finger holes), compared to the Scottish Great Highland bagpipe's single chanter, pointed downward, and multiple drone pipes, pointed upward. The *zampogna* is usually accompanied by a smaller, oboe-like instrument called a *piffero* or *ciaramella*, which plays the melody while the *zampogna* provides harmony and bass.

Beyond the technical differences, the sound of the Italian instrument inspires very different associations among its listeners than the Scottish bagpipe. Though the tradition dates back to ancient Rome, these days *zampogna* music is most likely to be played at Christmas, in part because it is considered a shepherd's instrument, with Italian legend maintaining that the music calmed the Virgin Mary during labor or that upon viewing the baby Jesus, the shepherds began playing as a tribute to the Christ child.

In central and southern Italy in particular, *zampognari* (bagpipe players), dressed in traditional shepherd's garb of short breeches and sheepskin vests with peaked caps, are a common sight beginning December 8—the Feast of the Immaculate Conception, and the official start of Christmas season. They proceed through the city streets, usually accompanied by an oboist, playing lullabies to images of the Virgin Mary and the baby Jesus. They may make stops at carpenters' shops, as a tribute to Joseph. These performances almost always include the popular holiday hymn "Tu scendi dalle stelle (Pastorale di Natale)" translated as "You come down from the stars (Christmas pastoral)," which musicologist Dick Spottswood calls "the Italian equivalent of 'Silent Night.'" They may also stop and play at carpenters' shops as a tribute to Joseph, and will make stops at individuals' homes (usually for a small donation).

SHOOTING IN CHRISTMAS: TAKING AIM AT EVIL SPIRITS IN THE SKY

BERCHTESGADEN, GERMANY

*T*he German district of Berchtesgaden, a scenic mountain municipality in the Bavarian Alps near the border of Austria, has some distinctive holiday traditions. In addition to being home to the Riddle-Raddle Men (see page 126), Berchtesgaden is also a place where on Christmas Eve each year, the sounds of carolers and sleigh bells give way to a rapid-fire series of noisy blasts. They are the cracks of about two hundred locals, high up in the hills, shooting off their rifles.

Such a high-caliber holiday celebration makes sense here: Berchtesgaden has a tradition of fine rifle-making dating back centuries. Every year on Christmas, each member of the numerous local shooting clubs grabs their *Handböller*—a vintage weapon that has to be hand-packed for each shot with black powder—and heads to the hills surrounding the German town. There, at precisely 11:30 p.m., they take aim at evil spirits and blast them from the sky for about half an hour. The shooting ramps up to a crescendo at midnight, at which point the sky falls silent, and the Berchtesgadeners know they had better get to midnight Mass. The people of Berchtesgaden repeat the practice all over again on New Year's Eve, with the shots serving as a kind of old-fashioned fireworks show.

Very old-fashioned, in fact: The tradition comes from an old pagan ritual, which holds that series of very loud noises during this time of year helps awaken nature from its winter slumber and frighten away evil spirits. In medieval times and earlier, this meant cowbells and a lot of yelling. Nowadays, it means lots of gunpowder.

While Berchtesgaden enjoys Shooting in Christmas, other parts of Germany and Scandinavia celebrate the tradition of Blowing in the Yule. Late on Christmas Eve, musicians grab up their brass Instruments and head to the local churches, blasting out joyful noise in every direction from the top of the church towers. It all leads up to midnight when the church bells take over, announcing that Christmas has arrived.

Croatia has its own holiday shooting tradition, with the men in each town taking to the streets at midnight on both Christmas Eve and New Year's Eve to shoot handguns into the air. Like in Berchtesgaden, it is said to help drive off evil spirits, though considering the proximity to other partiers, it's a bit more rambunctious than the German celebration.

PARANG MUSIC:
SINGING SPANISH ONCE A YEAR

TRINIDAD AND TOBAGO

*I*n the small island nation of Trinidad and Tobago, the primary language is English and the primary musical style is calypso, the soundtrack of the destination's annual Carnival. But this all changes in the lead-up to Christmastime. The steel drum gets put away, a four-stringed acoustic guitar called a *cuatro* comes out, along with some *shak-shaks* (maracas), and suddenly songs are being sung in Spanish, despite the fact that few people speak the language the rest of the year.

This is *parang*, the country's distinctive style of holiday folk music. Venezuelan and Colombian migrants historically sought farm work on the islands and brought these Spanish-language songs with them (the word *parang* derives from the Spanish word *parranda*, discussed at the beginning of this chapter). The songs grew popular, even among those who spoke little Spanish, and were soon adopted as standards to be sung at holiday gatherings and in homes.

Today, *parranderos* may schedule formal concerts or go door-to-door, sometimes playing whatever instruments they happen to find at each residence. In exchange, hosts will give them traditional treats such as the banana-leaf-wrapped *pasteles de masa* and holiday drinks like *ponche-de-crème*, the islands' answer to eggnog.

Parang fiestas and more formal competitions are hard to miss here during the holiday season.

Many participants sing the Spanish lyrics phonetically, while some *parang* groups will perform a pantomime along with the music so that even people who don't speak the language can understand. The popularity of the music has led to subgenres that blend in other local styles, such as the English-language, calypso-infused *soca parang* and the Indian-influenced *chutney parang*. As with most Christmas carols, the lyrics are mostly about the birth of Jesus, though they can incorporate secular topics as well—not that most of those listening can tell the difference.

MUMMERING:
SLIGHTLY TERRIFYING CHRISTMAS VISITORS

NEWFOUNDLAND AND LABRADOR, CANADA

*I*t sounds like something out of a horror movie: after dusk has fallen outside a rural home in chilly eastern Canada, the lonely person inside hears a pounding on the door. They open it to see a group of people with masked faces and oddly shaped bodies draped in rags. One speaks in a deep, distorted voice that is hard to even recognize as quite human, asking, "Any mummers 'lowed in?" and the person at the door feels like they had better answer yes.

In most situations, this would be terrifying. But if it is one of the Twelve Days of Christmas—between December 26 and January 6—and you happen to be in Newfoundland and Labrador, Canada's easternmost province, there is no need to worry; you are just being visited by the mummers. This practice first came to Canada with immigrants from England and Ireland during the seventeenth century but since then has developed into a ritual distinct to this province of fishing communities.

Covering their faces with scarves or crude masks and dressing in lumpy and ill-fitting clothing (borrowed from others to make them harder to identify), the mummers will usually play some fiddle music, sing songs, and challenge the person at home to guess their identities, speaking in strange voices to keep their audience from recognizing them. Men might dress as women and vice versa, wearing slippers as gloves or leggings on their arms.

The practice fell out of favor by the late nineteenth century, first as the mummers became more drunken nuisances than merrymakers (and a widely publicized murder of a local fisherman by masked men did not help), then as the local fisheries began to collapse, taking many communities with them. But janneying (another term for mummering) has experienced a resurgence in the last couple of decades. Towns have launched their own mummers' walks, and an annual Mummers Festival is now held in the Newfoundland city of St. John's. While it hasn't returned to the level of popularity it once enjoyed, mummering has solidified its place as a quirky part of Christmas in eastern Canada.

A pair of Newfoundland musicians are credited with helping resurrect the mumming tradition in the province, thanks to their 1983 tune "Any Mummers Allowed In?" (commonly called "The Mummers Song"). Bud Davidge and Sim Savoury, going by the band name Simani, released the catchy folk tune, which begins with a knock at the door and a shout of "Any mummers 'lowed in?" before descending into some high-energy fiddling and lyrics describing a granny being descended on by a group of mummers, whom the singer tries to identify while they all start a dance party in the kitchen before heading out.

It became a major Christmas hit and a staple of holiday radio throughout the region, spawning a children's book and serving as a soundtrack to renewed interest in the tradition.

LA GUIGNOLÉE:
TRICK-OR-TREAT FOR CHARITY

QUÉBEC, CANADA

A less jarring and more charity-minded door-to-door tradition can be found a bit west of Newfoundland and Labrador, in the Canadian province of Québec. Originating in medieval France, *la guignolée* is a custom of going to individual homes and asking for donations. In these early iterations, it was a true begging visit, where poor troupes of traveling singers beseeched the rich to give them food or drink for the winter holidays.

But over the centuries, as it was transported to North America during the French settlement in the seventeenth century, it became a more social tradition, allowing young people to spend time with each other on New Year's Eve. One constant was the begging song "La ignolée" (sample lyric: "All we ask—a pig's saddle roasted / No other dish. / But you can give us just as many, / As you may wish") and if the visitor asked that the host put a coin in their pocket, it was probably wise to oblige. Just like with trick-or-treating, the host would be playfully threatened that if they did not comply, they might be on the receiving end of a prank—and sometimes something more serious (another sample lyric: "If nothing to us, you would give, / Pray truly tell! / For then would we take away from you, / Your eldest girl.").

This custom is still practiced in Québec, where French is the primary language. Singers can dress up in traditional garb and sing for their own food and drink, or they can join up with a number of charities and not-for-profit organizations that use the night of *la guignolée* for legitimate fund-raising or as a food drive (now more likely to occur in late November rather than on New Year's Eve). Nonperishable food and funds are collected and prepared into "Christmas baskets" that are then donated to those in need. A version of *la guignolée* called *la guiannée* is also still observed in two American towns: Prairie du Rocher, Illinois, and Ste. Genevieve, Missouri. Both towns were founded by French Canadians.

Kids in Germany's Bavarian region have their own holiday ritual reminiscent of Halloween trick-or-treating: Knocking Nights (*Klopfelnachten*). Each of the three Thursdays leading up to Christmas, the children of the area put on frightening masks, grab up some noise makers (all the better to frighten off evil spirits) and go knocking on their neighbors' doors, reciting poems and receiving treats in return for their effort.

DEVIL'S KNELL:
INCESSANT STRIKES OF THE BELL

DEWSBURY, YORKSHIRE, ENGLAND

*I*n West Yorkshire, England, sits a picturesque little town called Dewsbury. The local Anglican parish church, Dewsbury Minster, dates back to the thirteenth century, and some of the original parts of the church are still there today. Every year on Christmas Eve, the church bells ring out the Devil's Knell, one ring of the bells for each year since Christ's birth. The ceremony is also called "the Old Lad's Passing Bell," a celebration of the banishment of the devil when Jesus was born and used to be widespread throughout England. But now, Dewsbury is the last place keeping the tradition going. The first year it took place here, the bell was rung 1,434 times, but it is now well past 2,000 rings. The last ring is set for midnight, so the Devil's Knell starts at around 10 p.m. nowadays.

The story of one of the minster's tenor bells is particularly interesting. The bell is named "Black Tom" after a knight named Thomas de Soothill. Supposedly, the knight found out that a servant boy had missed church the previous Sunday, so he hunted down the boy and threw him into the mill pond, where he drowned. As penance, de Soothill bought the church a new tenor bell, asking that it be rung on Christmas Eve. The church leaders must have been quite impressed, because they've certainly made use of the bell since then.

In the Swiss city of Ziefen, a few dozen young men dressed in dark coats and black top hats with large bells around their necks walk through the city streets at exactly 9 p.m. on Christmas Eve. They are led by the tallest of the bunch, wearing a fake white beard and carrying a pole with a sooty rag attached to the top—and none speak or sing, letting their bells announce their presence for them. But the bells are less remarkable than their headgear: the black top hats, made of black cardboard tubes, are comically tall, reaching as high as six feet above their heads.

Chapter 3

LOCAL QUIRKS

and

CURIOUS PRACTICES

For many cultures, Christmas opens up the opportunity to celebrate in ways very particular to a place, and that seemingly have little to do with the purported purpose for the holiday itself. From a frigid Christmas swim, to a dead bird propped on a pole, to a pooping log, here are some peculiarly local, and sometimes irreverent, ways that a number of places celebrate the season.

HOLIDAY BOOK FLOOD:
A TSUNAMI OF LITERARY GIFTS

ICELAND

*W*hether it takes place on Christmas Day, Saint Nicholas's Day, or Three Kings Day, gift giving has long been a central custom during the holiday season. But perhaps only on the Nordic island of Iceland can the giving of gifts be said to have helped maintain the national language. On Christmas Eve, family members and friends swap bound volumes with one another like trading cards. Some go out and buy a new book for each person on their list, working to pick just the right title. Or the family might get together and lay out a pile of books, letting each person select the one that catches their eye. However they're distributed, the popularity of giving books as gifts has earned the tradition the name Jólabókaflóð, or "Christmas book flood."

Here, the holiday season truly begins in early November when the Iceland Publishers Association catalog arrives at every household—literally, every household—in Iceland, providing a survey of all the new titles that can be ordered in time for Christmas. Orders pour in and the books start flowing.

In part, this is a reflection of Icelanders' dedication to cultivating their own language and culture (almost all the hundreds of titles in the catalog are in the Icelandic language—an astonishing output for a country of fewer than 350,000 people). The country publishes more books per capita than any other nation, with one in ten Icelanders having published a book themselves. At a time when the market for books has struggled, Iceland's publishing industry has proven resilient, thanks in part to the reliably powerful book flood each year. The custom partly grew out of World War II, when Iceland gained independence from Denmark. Many imported goods, including candy and toys, had been rationed during the fighting, but paper was one of the few that continued to flow freely.

To help spread the word of this literary tradition around the world, the nonprofit Jolabokaflod CIC campaign in support of books and literacy was formed in 2015, with the aim of bringing Iceland's bookish tradition to the wider world. They maintain that while gathering with loved ones is central to Iceland's holiday season, so is spending quality time with some new books.

CHRISTMAS SWIM: AN INVIGORATING START TO CHRISTMAS DAY

IRELAND

*D*ecember in Ireland is not exactly what you'd call "beach weather." Nonetheless, every year thousands of Irish men and women don swimsuits and Santa hats to leap into the frigid ocean water off the coast of the Emerald Isle. Although the tradition is only about forty years old, it has become a holiday institution in the country and continues to attract new participants every year. The swims now take place all along the coast at some of Ireland's most scenic (and chilly) spots. Many swims are sponsored by local sailing and swimming clubs, which provide mulled wine and hot chocolate afterward to those brave enough to take the dive. Participants raising money for local charities, or just doing it to prove that they can, pop on Santa hats (sometimes with silicone swim caps underneath, though wet suits are generally frowned upon) and take the dive.

Since cold shock can lead to hyperventilation and even cardiac arrest, the activity is truly not recommended for the faint of heart, and swimmers are encouraged to splash some cold water on themselves before taking the jump, to get acclimated to the chill. Considering the risks of diving into cold open water, most groups notify the Coast Guard and have medics standing by just in case.

CHRISTMAS SAUNA:
HEATING UP BEFORE CHURCH

FINLAND

*I*f hopping into freezing water does not sound appealing, you might find more to appreciate in how the Finnish people get into the Christmas spirit. As the temperature outside drops, Finns fight the frostbite by getting a steam at their local sauna. Participants gather in the birch hut, strip down, and pour a ladleful of water onto a pile of hot stones, releasing a pleasing burst of steam as they lie down on wooden benches and whisk one another with birch branches. On the afternoon of Christmas Eve, after the house has been prepared for the *yule* festivities, Finnish families will visit the sauna for a few hours of relaxation, cleansing, and warming of the body and mind. The saunas themselves are often specially washed in preparation for the holiday, with public saunas opening early on Christmas Eve day.

The sauna is a ritual here that dates back millennia, and is associated with the sacred, so it makes sense that the steam bath would be incorporated into midwinter festivities focused on peace and purification.

Following a lengthy sauna session, Finns will generally make their way to the local cemetery in the early afternoon (Finland gets dark early), candles in hand. After saying a few words, they will place the lighted candles by the graves of their loved ones, creating a warm Christmas glow as the flame reflects off the surrounding snow and joins with the many other candles left in the cemetery by other members of the community.

In Finland, Christmas is not just for the humans. Many Finnish families attach a sheaf of grain, seeds and nuts to the top of a pole and place it in their gardens and dub it the Birds' Christmas Tree.

BUMBA MEU BOI:
BRINGING BACK THE BULL

BRAZIL

*B*razil celebrates Christmas with a number of spectacles that encapsulate the diverse races and cultures that make up the country. These include door-to-door *reisados* dances based on Brazilian folktales during Folia de Reis (the Festival of Kings from December 24 to January 6), *pastoril* tales of shepherdesses on their way to find baby Jesus (complete with clowns, stars, and butterflies) and Rio de Janeiro's *Auto de Natal* play about the meaning of Christmas. But perhaps the most remarkable performance takes place in the rural northeastern part of the country, in the *Bumba meu boi*.

Translating to "Beating of the Bull," Brazil's *Bumba meu boi* festival is a sort of interactive play that takes place during the Twelve Days of Christmas (as well as in mid-June in some areas). Although the specifics of the story vary from place to place, the plot always centers on the death and resurrection of the titular bull. It is worth noting that no actual oxen are harmed in the performances—the bull is always played by one or more people in costume. Brazil is a huge country, and in the state of Maranhão alone, there are more than one hundred troupes that perform, each with its own distinct visual style and music.

A typical *Bumba meu boi* features a pregnant woman (played by a man) who must eat the tongue or liver of an ox in order to save her baby. A cowboy appears and sets out to find an ox, running into comical situations as he goes, before the animal is brought in to the cheers of the audience and does a dance. Then it is killed, and the audience and characters alike mourn the death of such an economically and culturally important creature. A number of different characters enter and try to save the ox, but they fail in humorous ways before the creature is finally revived and comes back to life. The audience cheers and the performers sing and dance.

The tradition originated in the late eighteenth century among cowhands and slaves, and the performances often include mockery of high-status characters. Doctors, priests, military men, and landowners all can serve as the punch lines of the comical episodes depicted over the course of the play, with the less-privileged characters outsmarting or overcoming their social superiors in various ways.

Brazil's gift bringer, Papai Noel, is almost indistinguishable from North America's Santa Claus, except he makes an arguably more dramatic entrance. In mid-December, tens of thousands of children gather in the massive Maracanã Stadium, singing Portuguese versions of Christmas standards as well as Brazilian carols such as "Repousa tranquilo, ó meigo Jesus" ("Lullaby for Baby Jesus") when a helicopter descends. As it lands, none other than Papai Noel pops out of it, waving at the thousands gathered and distributing gifts.

MARI LWYD:
CREEPY HORSE WITH
A PENCHANT FOR POETRY

WALES

*D*oor-to-door visits are a staple of Christmas celebrations across the globe, helping build community and bring individuals closer together during the holiday season. While they can take all types of forms—treating neighbors to carols, asking them for a charitable donation or some food, or incorporating them into a nativity scene—perhaps no such visit is as odd as Wales's Mari Lwyd, with its poetry-reciting horse skull on a stick.

Dating back to about 1800, the Mari Lwyd procession begins with a horse's skull with glass bottles for eyes, mounted on a pole and decorated with ribbons and bells, which is then draped in a white sheet so the person carrying it cannot be seen. At dusk, a party of four to seven men, dressed in clothes covered with colored ribbons, accompany the Mari Lwyd from house to house. Sometimes these men play distinctive roles such as a fiddler, Punch and Judy, or a leader who holds the horse's reins. At each house, the party sings a song requesting entrance, and the residents give as many excuses or hurl as many light-hearted insults, usually in verse form, as they can think of, taking part in a rhyme contest, or *pwnco*, that's something like a vintage Welsh rap battle.

Usually those inside the house relent and invite the interlopers in for food and drink. Not only is the zombie horse itself a bit unsettling to look at, but once inside, the Mari Lwyd may actually chase children around the home, trying to frighten them. For the most part, though, it's all just a bit of drunken fun before the horse and his crew move on to the next house.

Historians disagree on the origin of this somewhat frightening activity, with some suggesting it is rooted in a pre-Christian fertility ceremony and others maintaining it grew out of a medieval mystery play. But accounts of the traditions as they are practiced today go back only as far as the nineteenth century, when religious leaders wrote accounts of the nocturnal visits—in an effort to put a stop to them. Historians also have yet to agree on the meaning of the name itself, which has been translated as everything from "Holy Mary" to "merry games" to "gray mare."

While the practice is far less popular now than in its heyday, the creepy visage of the dead mare still makes annual appearances around Welsh villages or at holiday gatherings, such as the town of Chepstow's annual Wassail and Mari Lwyd, which attracts hundreds of visitors and a handful of dead horses each year. The cultural organization trac: Music Traditions Wales even sells a Mari Lwyd kit, complete with cardboard head, sheet, and instructions.

Similar hooded animal traditions can be found throughout the United Kingdom. The county of Kent's hoodening tradition places lighted candles in the eye holes and the "hooden horse" goes door-to-door asking for a gratuity (today, the money goes to charity). The Cotswolds' custom of the Broad would use a bull's head made of cardboard or stuffed skin, while Northern England's Old Tup would sport a goat's head.

TIÓ DE NADAL:
THE FRIENDLY POOP LOG

CATALONIA, SPAIN

*I*f a talking disembodied horse head seems like an odd Christmas tradition, how about a wooden log that poops out treats? In the Catalonia region of Spain, many families celebrate with a Tió de Nadal, or "Christmas Log," which is better described by its alias, Caga Tió—"Poop Log."

Starting December 8, the family puts out a hollow log, usually decorating it with a funny face and a red hat. (Though originally fashioned by each household from a wooden log, now it's more likely to be purchased from the store, complete with smiley face and stick arms on which it can be propped up.) The log is usually given a blanket to keep it warm during the cold winter nights. Each day, the children take turns "feeding" it by leaving water and scraps of food in front of it, which mysteriously disappear by morning. Finally, on Christmas Eve, they gently whack the log with sticks, singing a traditional song urging it to "poop" treats out.

The children may then be told to go somewhere else in the house to pray for Tió to deliver his presents (at which time their parents sneak the gifts under the blanket). They return to lift the blanket and find that the log has produced a pile of treats—typically small toys, nuts, sweets, and *turrón* nougat candy.

This odd tradition is believed to be rooted in a pagan winter solstice celebration traced back to the rural Pyrenees mountains, celebrating the earth's abundance. Then, as now, the celebration would usually conclude by tossing Tió on the fire as a symbol of rebirth, keeping the remaining ash in the home as a token of good luck for the year ahead. It might seem a harsh fate for a character who had produced so much holiday joy, but if anyone appreciates the importance of natural cycles, it would be a defecating log.

The Tió de Nadal has a number of its own songs, which kids sing on Christmas Eve as they hit the thing with sticks and try to get it to release its treats. One traditional song goes:

Caga Tió,	*Poop Log,*
caga torró,	*Poop nougats (turrón),*
avellanes i mató,	*hazelnuts and mató cheese,*
si no cagues bé	*if you don't poop well,*
et daré un cop de bastó.	*I'll hit you with a stick,*
Caga Tió!	*Poop Log!*

The Catalonians have another odd scatological Christmas tradition. Nativity scenes in the region often include an unexpected guest off in a corner of the manger, away from all the excitement around baby Jesus. It's a man dressed as a Catalan peasant in traditional *barretina* stocking cap, smoking a pipe and squatting with his pants around his ankles and his bare bottom exposed in the midst of defecating. That's El Caganer, otherwise known as "the crapper." Why would anyone want to put something so crude in the midst of such a sacred moment? Interpretations vary, with some saying his profane actions further elevate the sacred events happening around him; others see it as a reminder that we are all equally human. Whatever the reasons, the crapper has become essential to the Catalan nativity scene.

HUNTING THE WREN: RAISE HIGH THE DEAD BIRD

IRELAND AND ISLE OF MAN

*W*hile the UK celebrates December 26 as Boxing Day, Roman Catholics throughout Europe are more likely to consider the same date Saint Stephen's Day. Considered the first Christian martyr, Saint Stephen, who was executed for speaking against the authorities of the day, is honored with a public holiday in countries including Hungary, Switzerland, and the Philippines. In most of those places, it is celebrated with a feast or visit to church, but the Irish honor the day by sticking a fake bird on a pole and parading it around town.

Going back centuries, it was customary in the British Isles and France, on December 26, to kill and display a wren. Though the wren was considered "king of the birds" every other day of the year, on this date killing one was seen as a protective sacrifice. The bird would traditionally be stoned (morbidly appropriate, considering Saint Stephen was himself stoned to death), then affixed to the top a pole, with colorful ribbons and evergreen leaves as decoration. It would then be paraded around town before being plucked and buried, with its feathers sold as relics of good luck.

What did the wren do to deserve this treatment? Depends on whom you ask. In Ireland, it is sometimes said that when a group of Norsemen were about to ambush a Viking settlement, a wren beat its wings on the Norsemen's drums, alerting the enemy to their plan. Hunting the wren is a way to avenge this betrayal. A Manx version of the story claims that an enchantress once came to the Isle of Man and bewitched all the men and lured them into the ocean. But before she could be captured, she turned into a wren and flew away. Hunting the wren is a way of punishing her at last. More recent renditions of the tale connect the wren with the life of Jesus, making it a more fitting tradition during Christmas.

Either way, it was not a very pleasant fate for the bird. And over time the practice largely died out. However, in parts of Ireland as well as the crown protectorate of the Isle of Man, it has persisted, with a few significant reforms to make it a much less cruel ritual.

The songs and costumes that characterized the original rituals have returned, though now the "Wren Boys" have added women to their ranks. The procession and traditional dances are now likely

to be presented as a fund-raiser for charity or to preserve the old tradition. More important, live birds are no longer used in the proceedings. Celebrants may use a fake or taxidermy "wren" or simply a collection of ribbons or pair of hoops.

As the Wren Boys went about their parading, they would traditionally sing a "Wren Song" that went something like this:

The wren, the wren, the king of all the birds
On Stephen's Day was caught in a furze
Though he was little, his honor was great
So give us a penny to give us a treat.
My box would speak if it had a tongue
And two or three coppers can do it no wrong
Sing holly, sing ivy, sing ivy, sing holly
A drop just to drink it would drown melancholy.
And if you draw it of the best
I hope in heaven your soul may rest
But if you draw if of the small
It won't agree with the Wrenboys at all.
Missus you're a very fine woman
A very fine woman, a very fine woman
Missus you're a very fine woman
You gave us a penny to bury the wren.

FESTA DOS RAPAZES:
BOYS ON PARADE

PORTUGAL

*P*ortugal has its own Saint Stephen's Day celebration involving roving gangs of rowdy, costumed teenage boys. That would be the Festa dos Rapazes, or Festival of the Boys. The young men of each town (generally those around sixteen years old) take to the streets in brightly colored, fringed costumes, led by the *mordomo* or "steward"—a young man elected the previous Christmas to organize the event—who wears a special hat decorated with hanging red strips. Some carry sticks or bells and others play instruments such as rattles or cowbells, but each boy wears an elaborate mask of tin or wood to hide his face.

They may go door-to-door, soliciting donations for the church (or sausage, cheese, and wine for their own feast), gather around bonfires singing ancient chants, or "scare" the town's residents into the main square for a performance of music or a satirical skit and generally wishing the town happy holidays.

Throughout the festivities, the boys' home base is the Casa da Festa or "House of the Feast," where they meet, eat, and prepare for their various shenanigans. It leads up to the evening of December 26, when the boys gather for a celebratory feast at the Casa da Festa, where they stuff themselves on the donations of the locals and elect the *mordomo* for next year. Once dinner is finished, they head to a ball, where girls are allowed to join.

It should probably not be a surprise to learn that these festivities have pagan roots—in this case, connected to the worship of the sun god as well as rites of initiation that boys must pass to become men. It is not just a time for the young men of the town to run around and enjoy themselves, but a reminder of the region's ancient traditions and opportunity to reinforce the community's identity. As with many other pagan winter festivals, it has been tamed and Christianized over the centuries. Portugal is still a predominantly Catholic country, so once the day of running through the streets is over, the boys remove their masks and head to Mass, and are given the honor of being first to kiss the baby Jesus.

⛄
WINTERFEST:
A SECULAR SYMPHONY
OF LIGHTS

HONG KONG

*D*espite the fact that only a fraction of Hong Kong's citizens identify as Christian, the city's annual WinterFest may be one of the most eye-popping extravaganzas of the holiday season. That's because the whole month of December sees Statue Square in the middle of Hong Kong's central business district turned into a winter wonderland as part of the destination's WinterFest. Stores and other buildings string up millions of lights, choirs perform Christmas carols, and Santa even sets up a cottage. There are also many, many Christmas trees sprinkled with snow, with one giant tree erected in the center of Statue Square. Visitors can stop for a bite at one of the gourmet food vendors, catch a holiday ballet or concert, or take in the Symphony of Lights laser show, taking place every evening at 8 p.m.

All the festivities peak with a huge fireworks show over Victoria Harbour on New Year's Eve, which hundreds of thousands of spectators gather to take part in (336,000 attended the 2015 celebration alone, according to the Hong Kong Tourism Board). However, the celebrations don't end there. The traditional Chinese New Year falls at the end of January, so Hong Kong keeps most of the lights and decorations up all the way through February, replacing some of the Christmas decorations with lanterns. And, of course, the festivities stretch out to major theme parks like Hong Kong Disneyland, Ocean Park, and even Madame Tussauds wax museum. Christmas in Hong Kong is far from a religious experience, but the grandeur is hard to beat.

GOLDEN PIG:
A HALLUCINATION PROMISING
GOOD FORTUNE

CZECH REPUBLIC

*A*s in some other cultures, in the Czech Republic, it is traditional to fast the day before Christmas. Unlike in other cultures, however, practicing this discipline is supposed to provide
one with an intangible reward: If a person does not eat all day, he
or she will hallucinate a golden pig. The pig is expected to appear
on the faster's wall, and while it is not reputed to have much of
a personality, seeing it is considered a sign of good fortune and
prosperity.

These days, most Czechs do not fast completely on Christmas
Eve, but they do eat lighter meals in preparation for the feasts to
come. And the story of the golden pig continues to be referenced—
and is so well-known that it is the subject of a popular Czech soda
commercial in which a young girl asks her father to tell her the
story of the golden pig. For more than a decade, the humorous
ad has been trotted out every year, offering something of a Czech
version of those Coca-Cola polar bears. Whether they have fasted
or not, those who celebrate Christmas usually do so with a dinner
of fried carp and potato salad. As the children eat, they listen for
the sound of a bell. When they hear it, they know that Ježíšek (the
baby Jesus) has arrived and left presents under the Christmas tree.

Part 2

CHRISTMAS CHARACTERS

Chapter 4

SAINTS
and
GIFT BRINGERS

Santa Claus may be the best-known
holiday gift bringer on the planet, but he
is far from the only one. Many cultures assign
gift-giving duties to the Magi (see "Three
Kings Day" on page 18), but there are plenty
of more locally flavored characters sprinkled
across the globe. From a friendly witch to
a gregarious mountain giant to a flying baby,
countries around the world imagine
their bearers of holiday presents
in very different ways.

SAINT NICHOLAS/SINTERKLAAS: THE MANY VERSIONS OF THE MOST FAMOUS GIFT GIVER

NETHERLANDS AND BELGIUM

*J*f you picked up this book, it would be surprising if you were not familiar with the big-bellied gift bringer Americans know as Santa Claus. He captures our fascination and holiday excitement from a young age and has become the image of modern Christmas throughout the world. But the jolly man who is so central to Christmas celebrations has a number of counterparts in many other regions of the world who share many of his characteristics—yet are not quite the same.

Part of the reason for this complexity is the strange road that Santa has taken, evolving in different ways in different parts of the world, with the various versions of the character influencing one another.

These days, "Saint Nick" tends to be just one of Santa's nicknames (pardon the pun). But Saint Nicholas was a distinct figure that continues to shape celebrations in many parts of the world. The character has a history as long and luxuriant as his white beard, but he began as an actual human. A Christian bishop in the fourth century, he lived in the ancient Greek town of Myra (located in present-day Turkey). He had a reputation for generosity, with tales of him rescuing three sisters from a life of prostitution, saving innocent men from execution, and even resurrecting three young children who had been killed by an evil butcher and put in a pickle barrel.

For these various deeds, Nicholas was canonized and December 6 was declared Saint Nicholas's Day. His reputation as a bringer of gifts and kind figure toward children evolved into the practice throughout Europe of parents providing gifts to their kids in his honor, or slipping them into shoes as the children slept. As resistance to the Roman Catholic Church grew during Reformation in the sixteenth century, such veneration of saints was barred in many countries and the gift giving moved to December 24 and/or 25 or New Year's Day. The character of Saint Nicholas shifted to more localized gift bringers, rooted in regional lore, pagan rituals, or less Catholic elements of Christian belief. The thin, balding, and stern-looking fellow in bishop's robes was replaced by secularized versions of himself, kindly old women, or benevolent babies (more on them soon).

But while he was replaced by a wide range of characters, the Netherlands and Belgium continued to celebrate Saint Nicholas and still do today, as discussed in "Sinterklaas Festival" on page TK. Sinterklaas resembles his original saintly self, dressed like a bishop in a red cape and traditional miter headwear, carrying a crosier staff, wearing a ruby ring, and with a slimmer physique than his gift-bringing counterparts. He also continues to be celebrated on his original saint's day of December 6, which remains a bigger day of gift giving throughout the region than is Christmas. He rides a white horse named Amerigo or Ozosnel in the Netherlands, or Slecht-weer-vandaag in Belgium (which translates to "bad weather today") and is usually accompanied by his assistant Zwarte Piet (more about him on page 130).

For various reasons, whether to localize or secularize the character of Saint Nicholas, the character has been adapted into a number of other figures.

FATHER CHRISTMAS (ENGLAND)

The personification of Christmas cheer in England, this robed and bearded fellow appeared as early as the sixteenth century but didn't really take on his more familiar (and fatter) appearance until the late eighteenth century as interest in Christmas celebrations hit a new high. The specifics of his image vary, but the beard, fur-trimmed robe, and crown of holly were typical details and became solidified in the public imagination thanks to Charles Dickens's depiction of him as the Ghost of Christmas Present in *A Christmas Carol*. His rise during the Victorian era coincided with that of Santa Claus across the Atlantic, and he soon adopted the traits of his American counterpart. The character shifted from serving as a general symbol of merriment and holiday feasting to a gift bringer visiting homes to deliver goodies from his sack to eager children. Today, he's indistinguishable from Santa Claus beyond the fact that he is still often depicted as wearing a hooded robe, as opposed to Santa's short belted jacket.

PÈRE NOËL (FRANCE)

With a name that translates to "Father Christmas," it's not surprising that this character is partial to red fur-trimmed hooded robes, much like his English counterpart. But like the Netherlands' Saint Nicholas, he's a bit skinnier than Father Christmas or Santa Claus, and prefers to leave treats in shoes rather than hung stockings.

SAINT BASIL THE GREAT (GREECE)

While Saint Nicholas might be the historic holy figure most likely to be associated with holiday gift giving, in the Eastern Orthodox church, that distinction goes to Saint Basil the Great. This bishop of Caesarea Mazaca, located in present-day Turkey, is celebrated on January 1. Communities in Greece and southeastern Europe will celebrate Saint Basil's Day with gift exchanges, eating *vasilopita* ("Saint Basil cake," a sweet dessert with a coin hidden inside), and practicing the "Blessing of the Waters." Saint Basil plays the role of Santa Claus, leaving gifts for the children.

Two additional Santa lookalikes get a special focus in the next two sections: *Joulupukki* and *Ded Moroz*.

JOULUPUKKI:
A GENEROUS FELLOW WITH A WILD PAST

FINLAND

*T*he name of Finland's version of the jolly gift bringer translates to "Christmas goat," but to look at him, he seems not all
that different from a typical Santa Claus. The character generally
dresses in furs and boots, wears a beard, and travels from house
to house in a reindeer-drawn sleigh (though his reindeer aren't
reputed to fly, since often when he appears in reindeer-abundant
Finland, he is accompanied by the actual hooved animals). But he
didn't used to be so bland. Joulupukki previously lived up to his
name, wearing a mask and pair of horns and behaving more like
an animal. The character grew out of the Nordic *nuuttipukki* tradition in which people dressed as animals for fertility festivals or
other ceremonies and went from house to house asking for gifts.

These pagan festivities were absorbed into the kinder, gen-
tler Christmas celebrations, and the person going door-to-door
lost his troll-like character and began bringing gifts instead of
demanding to receive them. But he continued to be called "Christmas goat" despite no longer much resembling the animal, and to
ensure he bestowed treats on them, Norwegian children would
continue to leave barley grain in their shoes.

Things got even more complicated for the traditional character
when an official Santa Claus Village was built in the Finnish town

of Lapland. Since a much-publicized visit from China's then–vice president Xi Jinping (whose promotion to the presidency soon after is attributed in some quarters to his "lucky" visit here), Santa Claus tourism has exploded, particularly from China. Such market pressures have made it tough for Joulupukki to compete. But the goat has not totally gone out of the holiday. Decorative straw or wicker goats have become a common sight in many homes throughout the region (see "Yule Goat" on page TK), a tribute to its wilder holiday past.

If there can be a gift-bearing goat, why not a camel? While the camel-riding Wise Men are the traditional gift bringers for a number of cultures throughout the world, in Syria, it is one of the camels themselves that brings the presents. The legend goes that youngest of the three camels that brought the Magi to Bethlehem collapsed after the long journey. As it suffered exhaustion, the Christ child blessed it, granting it immortality.

This extraordinary creature is now said to carry gifts to the children of Syria, leaving them goodies on New Year's Eve (or making a black mark on their wrists if they have been naughty). To stay on the camel's good side, children will often leave out water and wheat to allow for refreshment on his rounds.

DED MOROZ & SNEGUROCHKA: THE GRANDFATHER-GRANDDAUGHTER HOLIDAY DUO

RUSSIA AND EASTERN EUROPE

*O*ne could easily confuse Ded Moroz for Santa Claus—the long white beard, the stocking cap, the bag of presents—but "Grandfather Frost," as his name translates in English, grew from the Russian folkloric tradition that those concerned about the winter chill should "invite the frost to supper," even setting out a meal for it. By the nineteenth century, the frost had been anthropomorphized into an actual character, particularly in the cities, where he was understood to live deep in the woods and oversee snow on the trees, ice on the river, and so on.

His reputation grew over the nineteenth century and efforts to appease Ded Moroz shifted from adults aiming to limit the seasonal chill by showing hospitality to the figure, to children, who were promised gifts from Grandfather Frost if they behaved themselves. He was said to travel in from the forest in his troika packed with gifts, often accompanied by another key character in Russian folklore: his helpful granddaughter, Snegurochka, or "Snow Maiden."

Snow Maiden has a rich mythology herself, appearing in folk tales throughout the nineteenth century. In one, which would go on to be adapted as a popular opera and films, she seeks to understand what human love is, but when Spring (another anthropomorphic character) provides that to her, as her heart warms, she melts. The character appeared in Christmas decorations throughout the late nineteenth and early twentieth centuries, but she did not begin to be referred to as a relative of Ded Moroz's until the twentieth century.

During the establishment of the USSR, the Communist regime banned the celebration of Christmas, including holiday characters such as Ded Moroz and Snegurochka. But over time, the empire's leaders decided that the celebration of the New Year would be acceptable, and so both figures were retrofitted in the Slavic countries that were then states in the Soviet Union—some of which had long celebrated Saint Nicholas or the Christ child as their local gift bringers—to fit the secular New Year celebration.

After the fall of the Soviet Union, both Grandfather Frost and the Snow Maiden would remain fixtures of Russia's winter celebrations, doing much of their work on New Year's Eve. But former Soviet states such as Ukraine and the Czech Republic brought back Christmas celebrations with gusto, returning the focus to Saint Nick and Christmas Day—and Grandfather Frost was sent back into the woods.

In 1998, Moscow's mayor declared that Grandfather Frost's home was the resort town of Veliky Ustyug, and a woodland residence for him was soon built, complete with sauna, winter sports facilities, and workshop—as well as a dedicated post office to answer children's letters to the gift bringer. But those in Belarus maintained that Ded Moroz was in fact from the Belarusian forest of Belovezhskaya Pushcha, and within a few years "Father Frost's Residence" had opened its doors, complete with a charming home and "throne room," Snow Maiden's tower, a Magic Mill that "turns bad things into dust and sand" and the Father Frost's Hut restaurant, serving up traditional Belarusian cuisine. By all accounts, both homes are well-trafficked with tourists.

In 2009, Russia launched a NORAD-like program to have their GLONASS (Global Navigation Satellite System) satellites "track" Ded Moroz and Snegurochka as they deliver their gifts.

☀
CHRISTKINDL:
GIFT-BEARING BABY

GERMANY

*A*lso known as Christkind or Christkindlein, this figure was initially introduced during the Reformation as a gift-giving alternative to Saint Nicholas. The story goes that Martin Luther himself explained that it was not a Catholic saint who brought children gifts during the holidays, but "Holy Christ," and the idea was taken literally. Originally envisioned as the Christ child himself delivering gifts, the Christkindl visited homes to both bless the family and generously leave behind presents for the children. In the process, he helped shift the seasonal gift giving from the Catholic feast day of December 6 to the celebration of the nativity on December 25.

Over time, the Christ child morphed into a more general messenger in angelic white robe and crown, usually played by a girl, sporting gold wings and a wand, serving more as a symbolic figure of holiday benevolence. It is also a character that now often appears in the flesh. Just as Santa Claus can be seen at malls or other holiday shopping spots, Christkindl often pays visits to the Christmas street markets in Germany, central to holiday celebrations (see *"Weihnachtsmärkte"* on page TK). Nuremberg's Christkindlesmarkt, the most famous of these fairs, is named after the character, and here a teenage girl, selected through a rigorous competition, dresses in gold and passes angelic blessings on to those visiting the market.

While Saint Nicholas is a prominent presence in Germany, asking children about their behavior and even taking requests for gifts, it is understood that he is not bringing the gifts himself, but taking the requests back to the Christkindl to fulfill.

Interestingly, as Santa Claus has grown in popularity as the gift-bringing figure throughout Europe, it has often been traditionalist Catholics who have urged the veneration of the Christkindl as a way of "restoring the true meaning of Christmas." It is a sentiment that would no doubt come to Martin Luther as a surprise.

When it reached North America, the word *Christkindl* morphed into Kris Kringle, becoming just one more name for the gift bringer with which Americans were far more familiar, Santa Claus. The book and film *Miracle on 34th Street* helped to popularize the name as an alias for the character.

Switzerland has its own tradition of celebrating Christkindl. On Christmas Eve in the area surrounding the village of Hallwil, a girl dressed in white robes and crown and veil walks through town carrying a lantern (in some cases she may be escorted by reindeer-drawn sleigh). She leads a procession of other children dressed in white, carrying baskets of gifts, which they distribute to Swiss children house to house. Some families may wait until the arrival of Christkindl before lighting the Christmas tree.

OLENTZERO:
GENEROUS MOUNTAIN GIANT

BASQUE

*A*lthough it is sandwiched between France and Germany, the Basque region is home to a language (also called Basque) distinct from both French and Spanish—and any other European language, for that matter. Believed by many to be the oldest ethnic group in Europe, the Basque people have traditions that are also distinctly their own, and that includes Christmas. Instead of Santa Claus, the Christkindl, or any other traditional gift giver, the Basques await a visit from a giant named Olentzero.

Olentzero's origins trace back to the sixteenth century, when he was said to be one of a race of mythical giants known as *jentilak* who lived alongside humans thousands of years ago. One day, these giants spotted a glowing cloud in the sky, and an old, nearly blind man told them it meant that Jesus had been born. Here's where the story takes a left turn: The old man and the giants were both terrified of Christianity, as they feared it would mean the end of their way of life. So the man asked the giants to take him to the top of a cliff and throw him off. They obliged, but as they headed back down, the giants tripped, fell from the cliff themselves, and died… all except for Olentzero.

Since then, the story has been toned down a bit. Other versions say that Olentzero was an orphan found in the woods by a fairy, who blessed him with strength and gave him to a childless couple who loved and raised him. He grew to be an accomplished wood carver, handing out wooden toys to the children of Basque Country. When he died, the fairy granted him eternal life, to be spent continuing to make children happy by bringing them toys.

In line with this version, Olentzero is usually seen nowadays dressed in the rough outfit of a Basque peasant, wearing a beret and smoking a pipe. Performers may dress like him at country festivals or share dolls and straw figures of the character. On Christmas Eve, some Basque children will make effigies of Olentzero and parade them through the streets, engaging in a yuletide version of trick-or-treat. In some regions, the evening ends with burning those effigies—symbolizing an end to the season, not any disrespect to the last of the mountain giants.

HOTEIOSHO:
AN ALL-SEEING PRIEST

JAPAN

*J*apan has vastly different cultural roots from the traditions that bring us Santa Claus, Saint Nicholas, or the many other gift givers. Nonetheless, Japanese children do have their own gift bringer. Hoteiosho is a god who's usually depicted as a Buddhist priest, wearing the open red robes of a monk. Like Santa, this figure has a big, round belly and a sack slung over his back, and he's sometimes even referred to as *Santa Kurosu*. But he also has eyes in the back of his head—the better to keep an eye on children and how they are behaving.

Hoteiosho is one of the seven gods of fortune in the Japanese pantheon, and fortunately, he's one of the nicer ones. As the god of happiness and abundance, he's always got a smile on his face, bringing cheer wherever he goes. Unlike Santa Claus, however, he's a wanderer with no North Pole to return to, and rather than ride in an opulent sleigh, he prefers to travel by foot.

Admittedly, it's a bit of a stretch to call him the Japanese Santa Claus, as there's little tradition of waiting for gifts from Hoteiosho on Christmas Eve. However, like Saint Nicholas, Hoteiosho—or Budai, as he's called in China—is partially based on a real person, a Chinese monk from the tenth century. You'll see statues of him all over Japan, and rubbing his belly is thought to bring one good luck.

Since Christians make up as little as 1 percent of Japan's population, Christmas is far from a major holiday in the country. The real gift giving here takes place during the New Year celebration, known as Shogatsu. During this time, the Japanese will thoroughly clean their houses and may place a straw rope known as a *shimenawa* and white paper strips called *shide* above the front door as a way to welcome the god of the New Year and keep out evil. Families gather together on Ganjitsu (New Year's Day) for feasting, games, and prayers, and parents will give *otoshidama* (decorative envelopes filled with cash) to their children. Who needs Hoteiosho when there's Mom and Dad?

FRAU HOLLE:
WELL-DWELLING WITCH

GERMANY

$\mathcal{F}$ather Christmas, Grandfather Frost, Saint Nicholas—what about the women in Christmas folklore? Check out Germany's Frau Holle. Also known as "Mother Frost" or "Mother Holda/Hulda," she's a holdover from pre-Christian pagan times—predating even Odin, Thor, and the rest of the Scandinavian pantheon—and plays an important role in the yuletide.

Instead of the North Pole, Frau Holle lives in a well, and instead of a sleigh, she drives a wagon. Like Diana from ancient Roman mythology, she's associated with nature and the hunt, and is depicted as flying across the night, accompanied by witches and the souls of the dead. She's known for her spinning or weaving, and in German Catholic folklore is associated with witchcraft.

In a tale bearing her name in Jacob and Wilhelm Grimm's collection of fairy tales, she bestows favor upon a virtuous girl and curses a lazy one, making her a bit like Santa Claus when it comes to keeping kids on their best behavior. Celebrated as part of Germany's midwinter festivities going back centuries, as the region embraced Christianity, she was folded into Christmas. During holiday celebrations in Alpine towns of Germany and Austria, many will don a Holda mask.

Frau Holle is celebrated in wintertime in part due to her position as goddess of death and regeneration—in order to bring new life, the old must die. Each year, she blankets the world with snow (the winter snowfall is depicted in fairy tales as Frau Holle churning up feathers while fluffing her pillow or making her bed), but then rebirths it each spring. At least those feather pillows must bring some homey comforts to the bottom of a well.

LA BEFANA:
THE BENEVOLENT CHRISTMAS WITCH

ITALY

*L*a Befana, also known as the Christmas Witch, is not quite as intimidating as Frau Holle and shares more in common with Santa Claus (known as Babbo Natale in Italy). She delivers her presents on the night before Epiphany (January 5), and if anything, her story is more closely connected to the Bible than that of the jolly fat man up in the North Pole. The story goes that on their way to Bethlehem, the Three Wise Men approached an old woman who was sweeping her house and asked her directions to where the Christ child might be. She did not know, but she provided the Magi with shelter for the night. The next day, they invited her to join them in their search. She turned them down, saying she was too busy with her housework. But as soon as they left, she had second thoughts, grabbed up some gifts for the newborn, and set out to catch up with them.

She did not reach them in time, and according to folklore, she continues the search to this day, popping down chimneys on Epiphany ("Befana" derives from "Epiphania") and leaving gifts in stockings for the good children she finds along her path. Like Santa, La Befana gets letters from children describing the gifts they want, and she also leaves hunks of coal for those children determined to be naughty.

But despite her association with the Christmas season, La Befana has also gained some witchy qualities—she's often depicted as a crone in a kerchief, speeding up her travels by riding on her broomstick. Originally, La Befana was a character specific to Rome, but now all of Italy as well as Italian communities in the U.S. hang their stockings out for the Christmas Witch.

La Befana has gained popularity beyond Italy. She has a Russian counterpart in Baboushka, with the same backstory and appearance. And then there's Germany's Frau Perchta, who shares many similarities, though she also has a habit of sneaking into bedrooms to rock children to sleep. France's Tante Arie ("Aunt Arie") fills this role for the Franche-Comté region. She's said to come down from the mountains to deliver presents for good children and dunce caps for naughty ones, and can usually be spotted at the Mont-béliard Christmas market, dressed in the modest clothing of a peasant, accompanied by a donkey loaded with gifts.

Chapter 5

DEVILS

and

TROUBLEMAKERS

If it is not clear already, Christmas has a dark side. Many of the feasts, gifts, and good cheer that rule the holiday were first developed centuries ago as a way to alleviate the cold, darkness, and other miseries of midwinter—some of which took the form of sinister characters and devils. While North America has managed to expel these darker aspects, they remain alive and well in Europe and elsewhere, particularly in the strange companions and fiendish characters who pop up alongside the friendly gift bringers associated with the holiday. Here are a few of these Yuletide troublemakers.

KRAMPUS:
THE CHRISTMAS DEVIL

AUSTRIA

*K*rampus is half goat, half demon, with horns, a long forked tongue, and one cloven hoof and one human foot. He follows Saint Nicholas around as he gives his gifts to the good children. Krampus's job is to punish the naughty kids, using a whip or bundle of birch switches. In some depictions he wears a basket on his back, into which especially bad children will be tossed and taken to his underworld lair. While he may be frightening, Krampus is a cherished character throughout Austria and Bavaria and can be found on Christmas cards, figurines, and sweets, and a celebration is held in his name every December 5.

That is not to say that Krampus has always been widely beloved—children are not the only ones who have found him frightening. His roots date back to pre-Christian paganism, and during the twelfth century, the Catholic Church tried to banish Krampus celebrations. He persisted as a generalized bogeyman, varying in appearance by region. By the mid-nineteenth century, he had evolved into the modern version of the character that we recognize today. Austria's Fascist rulers of the 1930s prohibited the presence of the Krampus due to their belief that he represented anti-Christian values.

But the Christmas devil has outlasted all his enemies and has only grown stronger in the process. In recent years, Krampus has made a major comeback, with Krampusnacht, or "Krampus Night" (taking place December 5, the eve of Saint Nicholas's Day) becoming an increasingly popular affair every year. Austrians decked out in Krampus outfits and elaborate masks take to the streets for an unruly parade, ringing cowbells, playfully frightening onlookers, showing off their costumes, and celebrating the more sinister side of Christmas. The character has been embraced internationally, with cities like New Orleans and Washington, D.C., throwing their own Krampus parties, or Perchtenlaufen processions.

Though Krampus is the most prominent of the Christmas demons, there are plenty of other similarly sinister companion figures known by a range of names with only slight differences in appearance or practices. German-speaking parts of Europe have been especially prolific in developing these characters, with a different devil for seemingly every town, each with his own specific characteristics and nasty habits. A few Christmas companions:

Knecht Ruprecht: His name translates to "servant Rupert," and he originated as something of a manservant to Saint Nicholas. He tends to dress in a long coat of animal skins and wears a long, messy beard, and takes over the quizzing of children about their behavior, whether they pray, and if they have been naughty. In Germany, he is the most familiar of the holiday sidekicks and may go by Hans Ruprecht, Rumpknecht, or a number of other names.

Pelznickel/Belsnickel: This figure is partial to tattered furs and carrying a switch to use on naughty kids. He originated in the Rhine region and continues to make appearances around southwestern Germany (as well as parts of Pennsylvania with large populations of German immigrants).

Rû Clâs ("Rough Nicholas"): Most popular in the northern German region of Mecklenburg, this guy also is just as he is advertised: a disheveled, messier companion to Saint Nicholas who does the saint's dirty work for him.

čert: Literally translating to "Devil" in Czech and Slovak cultures (and known as Çor in Turkish), this character generally dresses in black and carries a whip, chains, and a sack to toss children into if they've been misbehaving. He, along with a white-clad Anděl ("angel"), accompanies Svatý Mikuláš (Saint Nicholas) as he descends from the heavens on a gold cord. The trio parades through the streets, giving out treats or threatening punishments.

Père Fouettard ("Father Whipper"): Said to be the butcher from the Saint Nicholas legend who chopped up three boys and tossed their remains in a pickle barrel (see "Saint Nicholas/Sinterklaas" on page TK), this figure now joins France's Père Noel as he makes his rounds. Partial to long, dark robes and an unkempt gray beard, Père Fouettard will take care of the punishment of naughty children, threatening to chop them up and eat them if they've misbehaved.

Hans Trapp: A bogeyman of the Alsace region of France, legend has it that he was once a rich, greedy man who was exiled to the surrounding forest. There, he disguised himself as a scarecrow to prey on children and continues to come for the naughty ones.

THE YULE LADS AND GRÝLA: A ROWDY CREW OF MOUNTAIN-DWELLING PRANKSTERS

ICELAND

*I*magine a scary holiday version of Snow White's seven dwarves—except that there are thirteen of them and instead of Sneezy and Sleepy they go by names like Stubby and Meat Hook—and you are starting to get a picture of Iceland's Yule Lads. These characters are said to descend from the mountains one by one on the nights preceding Christmas playing pranks on the local children and creating general mayhem.

They are a rough-looking lot, each wearing a beard, ragged clothes, and a red cap, resembling a mischievous gnome or elf on a bad day, with names that reflect the particular type of havoc they bring to Icelandic households: Spoon Licker, Window Peeper, Bowl Licker, Candle Stealer, and Sausage Swiper, to name a few. But once their nightly disturbances are done, the lads may leave a small gift in children's shoes—or a rotten potato for those who have been naughty.

However, it is not this rowdy crew that Icelandic children fear, but the Yule Lads' mother, Grýla. A cruel ogress living in a cave in Iceland's hinterlands, she is said to come out of hiding each year during the holidays to snatch up naughty children and whip them into a stew in her giant pot. She is usually joined by her husband

and accomplice, Leppalúði, and her Yule Cat, a giant black feline that is known to gobble up children who do not receive a new piece of clothing during the holidays. (Why it is the children's fault that their parents failed to get them new clothes is left unexplained.)

As unpleasant as this group might seem, Icelanders have an enduring affection for them, and their legends have persisted for centuries. Stories of Grýla date back to the fourteenth century (though she was not connected to Christmas until the 1800s, when the Yule Lads and Yule Cat entered the picture). She embodies the looming threat of winter in a place known for its harsh conditions as well as an effective way to keep children from misbehaving.

While attempts have been made to sanitize and "Santa-fy" these characters in recent years, turning them into gift-bringing figures more than holiday devils, Icelanders and their cultural institutions have pushed back, determined to keep their folklore uniquely weird. So far, Grýla and her brood look like they will be scaring kids—and licking bowls, stealing candles, and all the rest—for many years to come.

Iceland is not the only Scandinavian country with troublemaking elves. The *nisse* of Norway and Denmark and *tomte* of Sweden and Finland look quite a bit like garden gnomes, with their short stature and conical hats, and they are known to show themselves around the winter solstice and Yuletide. They are traditionally protectors of farms and livestock (*tomte* translates to "homestead man"), but are not above stealing from neighboring farms and are known to mete out small punishments for what they view as rude behavior. If you swear, spill things, or anger the livestock, you had better leave a bowl of porridge out so these sprites do not wreak havoc in the barn or tie the cows' tails together. During the Christmas season, *julenisse* may accompany the Yule Goat (see "Joulupukki," page TK) to hand out presents.

──☆──
KALLIKANTZAROI:
TREE-CHOPPING
CHRISTMAS GOBLINS

GREECE, BULGARIA, AND SERBIA

*T*he characters of Greek folklore may not be as familiar as the gods and heroes of ancient Greek mythology, but they have plenty of fascinating stories of their own. One prominent example: the Christmas-loving goblins known as *kallikantzaroi*. As the legend goes, the world and the heavens are both supported by a colossal tree with its roots penetrating down into the underworld. All year, *kallikantzaroi* are hard at work attempting to saw through the trunk of the World Tree and make all of it collapse. However, just as they are about to succeed in severing it, Christmas arrives, and the goblins are allowed to pop up aboveground into the mortal world (in a number of pagan traditions, the boundary between the physical and spiritual worlds was believed to open, or be at its weakest, during winter solstice).

Here, during the Twelve Days of Christmas, they are said to have so much fun playing pranks on humans that they forget all about the tree. When the Christmas celebration is over, marked by the Blessing of the Water during Epiphany (see page 18), they are forced back down into the underworld. When they get there, they realize that the joyful celebrations have in fact healed the World Tree and their work must begin again. The rascals are forced to start over for another year, and they will not be seen again until the next December.

It's a charming tale of the healing power of the holidays. But in Greece and the surrounding southeastern European countries, the subterranean goblins are also believed to cause problems during their time above ground. They come down people's chimneys and perform such irritating mischief as souring milk, peeing on the fire, or breaking the furniture. To keep them away, families are urged to try a number of Christmas Eve rituals, such as burning a Yule log, marking the house door with a black cross, or hanging pork bones in the chimney. If that doesn't work, they can try burning their smelliest shoe or leaving a colander at the doorstep. The *kallikantzaroi* will feel compelled to count all the holes, but since they can't count past three (a holy number), they will never finish.

Some German-speaking regions also maintain that the twelve days of Christmas (the nights in particular) are a period when the boundary between the natural and supernatural worlds break down. Some towns call them "between-nights" or "under-nights," while other call them "knocking nights" in reference to the bands of masked young people who go door to door making noise and demanding treats. In other parts of Germany, they are known as "smoke nights," in reference to the burning of incense and building of bonfires that once took place during this time.

BUTTNMANDL:
FRIENDLY NEIGHBORHOOD
RIDDLE-RADDLE MEN

BERCHTESGADEN, GERMANY

*L*ocated in the Bavarian Alps, Berchtesgaden celebrates Saint Nicholas's Day as its primary gift-giving holiday—and like in many other areas of Germany, the holiday's namesake has some odd helpers accompanying him. The Running of the Riddle-Raddle Men offers a rambunctious twist to the big holiday. Before Saint Nicholas himself can march through the town, these guys—carrying switches and dressed in scary masks with sheaves of straw tied around their bodies, forming a rough star shape—clear his path, yelling and clanging cowbells or other noisemakers.

The idea is that their frightening appearance and clatter will scare away any evil spirits that may be hanging around (even though they seem more than a bit nasty themselves). With the path open, they must then be blessed by Saint Nicholas (or a farmer's wife, dousing them with holy water) so that they can accompany him as he goes from house to house, handing out gifts or leading the locals to bonfire ceremonies and other community gatherings.

Traditionally, it is the young men of the town who don the Riddle-Raddle costumes, waking up before dawn to gather in a barn, hand-threshing the straw for their outfits and preparing for the festivities. The celebrations can take on a more charged, if play-ful, form as the raddlers behind the masks chase after not just demons but their girlfriends or the local ladies on whom they have crushes. No surprise that the practice originated as a type of fertility ritual—though now it is seen as just a bit of silly holiday flirting.

DANCING DEVILS: RAMBUNCTIOUS HOLIDAY GIFT TAKERS

LIBERIA

*M*any cultures have the character of the kindly old man who gives out gifts at Christmastime, but Liberia has inverted the concept with its "dancing devils"—a group of costumed characters that descend on towns and markets throughout the African country during the holidays. These figures are not here to give presents, but to request them.

Dressed in layers of brown raffia straw and colorful masks, accompanied by drummers and sometimes walking on stilts that allow them to tower over those below, these characters can be both fun and frightening. They parade through Liberia's streets, dancing and playfully spooking children. They go door-to-door with their hand or raffia hat held out, requesting a donation or gift of some kind. Money is always appreciated, but sweets or cold beer will do just fine, too.

The characters are essentially street performers who have blended Western Christmas elements with traditional African dance and the "bush devil" figures that have long been a staple of local mythology and festivals. Their performances and entertainment are viewed as a kind of gift in themselves, so it is quite reasonable that they expect to be compensated for the effort.

A few of these devils have distinct identities, such as Old Man Bayka, or "Old Man Beggar," in piebald clothing, walking up and down the streets, usually alongside Santa Claus (though a distinctive Liberian take on the character). These characters, along with a Speaker serving as master of ceremonies, may perform local songs ranging from "Merry Christmas, We Are at Your Door" to "Young Girl, Stop Drinking Lysol," leading crowds in a call-and-response chant and performing special dances. Old Man Beggar might also offer up some social commentary or message of Christian morality. But he can be counted on to include a request for gifts in the form of the line "My Christmas is on you."

Liberia is not the only West African country with Christmas devils. The tradition is practiced throughout the region with local variations. For example, Sierra Leone is home to Jobai, a small-headed character that does a spinning dance, as well as Gogoli, sporting an unusually large head.

ZWARTE PIET: SINTERKLAAS'S CONTROVERSIAL COMPANION

NETHERLANDS

*Z*warte Piet, or Black Peter, originated in Dutch folklore as a helper for Sinterklaas. But these days, he is more often the source of difficulties than he is of assistance. The character first appeared in a mid-nineteenth-century children's book that laid out many of his defining characteristics. He wore the colorful costume of a Renaissance-era page (short pants, stockings, and a cap with a large feather), harking back to the Spanish occupation of the Netherlands. He was also said to be a "Moor" (an old term for Muslims who lived in the Iberian Peninsula) from Spain who had dark skin.

Specifics about his origin vary, with some saying he was a slave rescued by Saint Nicholas, others that he was a former devil but now has turned to doing good. But as celebrations of Sinterklaas became more elaborate, including the gift bringer arriving by boat to Amsterdam, Antwerp, and elsewhere, Zwarte Piet became a constant presence by his side, handing out presents from an over-size sack he carried and also delivering lashings when they were merited. Compared to some of the other companions of Saint Nick, Black Peter is perhaps the most amiable. But his portrayal, often by a white person made up in blackface, stirs up controversy that only grows with each passing Christmas season.

The backlash to Zwarte Piet has come to a head predominantly in the Netherlands, where some see him as a cartoonish stereotype and others point out that the power dynamic between Pete and Nick is all but an endorsement of the slave trade—and that it is never appropriate for a white person to be donning blackface today, regardless of cultural context. But these protests have hardly swayed the Dutch, with more than 90 percent in one recent poll stating that they supported a traditional version of Black Peter.

While large majorities in the Netherlands do not view Zwarte Piet as a racist figure, there has been less patience for the character in former Dutch colonies where Sinterklaas celebrations continue. Curaçao's prime minister has criticized the character and today Peter is more likely to appear with his face painted rainbow colors. Officials in Suriname have called for a ban on Sinterklaas celebrations altogether. So far, the parties continue, but Zwarte Piet's role in the festivities diminishes each year.

Spain, the supposed homeland of Black Peter, has recently faced its own challenges regarding Christmas characters in blackface. The Magus Baltasar in the Three Kings Day procession taking place in cities across Spain has for decades been portrayed by a blacked-up white person. For Madrid, that changed in 2015, when the city authorities announced that the character would from that season forward be portrayed by an actual black person. Many other Spanish cities have followed Madrid's lead in banning the blackface.

Part 3

FUN AND
FEASTS

Chapter 6
HOLIDAY TRIMMINGS
and
TRINKETS

For many, the holiday season officially begins when the box of decorations comes out of storage, and whether that means setting up elaborate light displays or setting out simple ornaments or quirky family heirlooms, these serve as tangible symbols of Christmastime. But the kinds of decorations and objects that symbolize the season in different countries vary as much as Christmas traditions themselves.

NATIVITY SCENES: CREATIVE CRIBS

EUROPE

$\mathcal{S}$ ome historians trace the practice of creating and staging the scene of Jesus's birth site to Saint Francis of Assisi, who was described setting up a manger in the year 1223 in a cave in the small Italian village of Greccio. Whether he was in fact the first to come up with the idea is questionable, but the practice goes back at least that far, and the idea of staging the Bethlehem scene, either in miniature or life-size, has become a central part of Christmas throughout the world.

Assisi's early version was rough by today's standards—just a couple of hay bales and a live ox and donkey, not a person or Christ child to be seen. But the design of these crèches, as nativity scenes are also known, has come a long way from there, spreading throughout southern Europe, Latin America, and beyond, first as live scenes with actors, then as static scenes that could be displayed and transported more easily. More effort went into the design. More characters were added—not just the Holy Family, but entire villages of people as well as curiosities of the local culture. And the scale grew until some stretched dozens of yards, seeming to form their own entire cities.

Certain countries, regions, and individual towns take their own unique approaches to the practice, infusing it with their local culture and folk art traditions. Whether it's a *portal*, *jeslicky*, *belen*, *Kripp*, or *pesebre*, the scene is not just an expression of religious observance or holiday celebration, but of the specific culture from which it sprouts.

A few nativity traditions from around the world are:

Betlémy (Czech Republic): Nativity scenes trace back to the sixteenth century in this region, though they did not begin appearing in homes until at least the eighteenth century. What sets the Czechs apart from other makers of nativity scenes is their breadth. The scenes extend beyond the stable and the traditional characters, incorporating the wider surroundings of everyday life in Bethlehem, with farmers, craftsmen, traders, and musicians joining in the celebration of the Christ child. No wonder they refer to these not as "cribs" or "mangers" but by the more expansive Betlémy, or "Bethlehems."

This art form has such a rich history here that one can find multiple museums dedicated to the craft, including the Museum of Nativity Scenes in Karlstejn, outside of Prague (with more than fifty scenes, some made of sugar, bread, and coconut shells), and the Třebechovice Museum of Nativity Scenes, about one hundred miles east. One highlight of the latter is the scene by Josef Probošt, first begun in the late nineteenth century, which took four decades to complete. The delicately carved wooden sculpture measures almost twenty-three feet wide and more than six feet deep, including more than two thousand carved pieces, with 373 people—put in motion by an electrical motor.

But to see perhaps the most stunning work of nativity art in the Czech Republic, one should head south to the Bohemian town of Jindřichův Hradec, where a museum exhibits the largest mechanical nativity scene in the world—Tomáš Krýza's nearly 1,400-figure masterwork (of which 133 characters move), stretching more than fifty-five feet, which took more than sixty years for the craftsman to complete.

Szopka (Krakow, Poland): Poland may be the Czech Republic's neighbor, but the approach to nativity scenes there could not be more different. Rather than the wooden hues of the Betlémy, the *szopka* of Krakow are brightly colored castles that stretch much higher than they do wide. These elaborately decorated scenes often include a detailed miniature of the city's distinctive Gothic and Renaissance architecture, including recognizable structures like the Wawel Cathedral.

These scenes serve as a theater backdrop to the Holy Family and characters from local legends, often represented with moving figures or puppets. Regional costumes and the eagle ensign of Poland add a local accent to the works. Colorful tinfoil, cardboard, and even candy wrappers are used in the construction and displayed in the city center as part of an annual contest for the best decorated scene. Each year on the first Thursday of December, the Historical Museum of the City of Krakow hosts the crèche-building competition in Krakow's main square. But as detailed as they may get, these pieces are lighter weight than they may appear. Having developed out of a tradition in which they were carried from door to door as a portable theater on which to display nativity plays, the *szopka* are meant to be mobile.

⁃

Santons (Provence, France): A home in this region is not ready for Christmas without a striking crèche at its center. And no Provençal nativity is complete without a few figures beyond the usual Holy Family, Three Kings, and baby that one would expect. Among these bonus characters: a baker, a fishmonger, a water carrier, and a mayor—and potentially dozens of other village folk—made of hand-painted baked clay. These are the *santons*, or "little saints," and are a distinct practice in this region that grew out of the French Revolution, when Catholic churches were closed and nativity scenes forbidden. Crèche-making moved indoors and became much more of a DIY affair. *Santon* making has since become a respected craft, with more than one hundred family-run workshops throughout the region and a small Musée du Santon.

⁃

Presepji (Malta): Known as *presepji* ("cribs"), nativity scenes in the Mediterranean archipelago of Malta depict a more expansive and distinctly Maltese scene than the traditional gathering of Holy Family and Wise Men. These include landscapes, buildings, flour windmills, and other elements inspired by local imagery—as well as a large baby Jesus figure as the centerpiece, though he often is not placed there until Christmas night. But the uniquely Maltese addition to the nativity is vetch sprouts, or *gulbiena*—stringy white tendrils that work well as the hay or straw for the manger scene. The vetch seeds are sown on cotton buds in flat pans, planted about five weeks before Christmas (December 7 is usually the preferred day for planting in order to ensure readiness by the Orthodox Christmas of January 6) and sprout up white, though they turn dark when exposed to light for long periods. These days, vetch is worked into secular Christmas decorations as well, since it makes an ideal beard for Santa.

YULE GOAT:
A COMBUSTIBLE CHARACTER

SWEDEN

*W*hile reindeer might be the animals that North Americans most closely associate with Christmas, in Sweden, that honor goes to the goat. *Julbock* ("Yule buck") decorations are ubiquitous, whether as life-size figures at the entrance of holiday markets or small ornaments hanging in a family Christmas tree. While they come in all sizes, a *julbock* (known in Denmark and Norway as *julebukk*) is generally made of straw wrapped with red ribbon into the shape of a goat, complete with braided horns and a few sprouting whiskers.

While the goats have a harmless, even friendly appearance, the origin of the *julbock* is a bit darker. Some claim the Yule Goat tradition comes from the worship of Thor, who supposedly rode a chariot pulled by two goats, which could be cooked up and eaten for dinner...and return to life the next day to continue on their course. But the connection between goats, the end of the harvest, and the beginning of winter more likely relates to pagan midwinter festivals in which a person dressed like a goat, usually demanding gifts, as a representative of various devilish figures. If treats were not forthcoming, the goat could be expected to crash around, kicking up trouble and destruction.

Over time, the character's place in festivities shifted. Sometimes a goat would be placed in a neighbor's yard as a prank; other times, raucous groups of singers would take to the streets singing holiday tunes, with at least one dressed as a goat. The Yule Goat took on the role of Santa, with the family gift bringer dressing up as the character to distribute gifts to family or friends. Nowadays, as Santa has spread throughout Scandinavia, the *julbock* is far more likely to appear in straw, rather than human, form (see "Joulupukki" on page 98).

But that's not to say the figure has been sidelined during holiday celebrations. In the city of Gävle, Sweden, the town's citizens have erected a massive *julbock* in Castle Square every Christmas since 1966. While the locals love it, within the first few years, the highly combustible creature mysteriously ignited. It was not determined whether the fire was an accident or the result of foul play, but it was not long before it happened again . . . and again. The giant goat would burn more than thirty times in the next five decades, in spite of elaborate efforts from the people of Gävle to protect their local mascot: security cameras and fences, flameproof chemical sprays, and even guards.

It has required the goat's foes to get creative: In 2005, a group of people dressed as Santa and gingerbread men fired flaming arrows at it from a distance. In 2009, hackers deactivated the cameras and snuck into the goat's cage to light it on fire. In 2001, an American tourist spent two weeks in a Swedish prison for trying to set it aflame, telling authorities his Swedish friends had told him it was okay. In 2016, the fiftieth anniversary of the goat's intro-duction, it was celebrated in an elaborate festival . . . and burned down that night. Intentionally or not, the annual prank serves as a tribute to the Yule Goat's troublemaking origins, adding a bit of anarchy and theatrical destruction to the best-laid holiday plans.

PARÓL:
LANTERNS LIGHT THE WAY

*A*s a predominantly Catholic country, the Philippines pulls out all the stops when it comes to Christmas. The official Christmas season includes the nine-day series of Masses known as Simbang Gabi, beginning December 16, and lasts until Epiphany. But as early as September, it is not unusual to see star-shaped lanterns dotting the streets or appearing in windows or above doorways.

This is the *paról*, the country's famed Christmas decoration that is as ubiquitous during the Filipino Christmas as the Christmas tree is in the U.S. Introduced during the Spanish regime (the word comes from *farol*, the Spanish word for "lantern" or "light"), they served as a method of public lighting, illuminating the way to Mass for those in rural areas, sometimes carried by congregants or posted on the path along the way.

Originally made from bamboo and thin *papel de japón* (rice paper), they started shaped as simple rectangles or ovals and became more elaborate over time. Today, with sometimes intricate decorations, they may take the form of animals, or the most popular star shape with lacelike cut-paper "tails" hanging from their points. Referencing the Star of Bethlehem that guided the Three Kings to Jesus's manger, it became a powerful symbol for the triumph of light over darkness and literally as the tool that lit the way to church for many. Their three-dimensional shape allows for a candle (or, now for safety reasons, a small lightbulb) to be placed inside of them. More recently, they're made with wooden sticks or wire and cellophane that allows light to pass through them. *Paról* making is a regular activity in Filipino homes during the holidays, and many villages, schools, and other communities hold competitions to see who can make the best lantern.

The city of San Fernando, dubbed the "Christmas Capital of the Philippines," is where many of the country's Christmas lanterns are produced and plays host every year to the Giant Lantern Festival. Teams of builders compete with one another, creating nearly twenty-foot-wide lanterns, placing thousands of bulbs on a welded steel frame (the competition limits the number of lights per participant to ten thousand), connecting them with system of hand-controlled switches (along with plenty of hairpins and masking tape—no computers are allowed). Colored plastic or fiberglass is precisely cut and wrapped around each part, creating a massive *paról* that offers its own self-contained light show.

PŌHUTUKAWA: KIWI CHRISTMAS TREE

NEW ZEALAND

Since Christmas falls during the summer in New Zealand, Kiwis tend to celebrate things a bit differently, with beach barbecues, outdoor events, and a Santa who wears sunglasses and sandals. So it makes sense that the Christmas tree here also looks a bit different from the conifer of colder climes. In New Zealand, the beloved holiday evergreen is the pohutukawa, a dome-shaped tree that erupts with red blossoms between November and January, complementing its dense branches of green leaves. The trees grow on the rocky cliffs of New Zealand's northern coast, but during the holidays they can be seen on Christmas cards, retail displays, and domestic Christmas decorations.

Beyond its natural beauty and Christmassy colors, the tree is viewed with special significance by New Zealand's native Maori people, whose mythology holds that the red blossoms represent the blood of a young warrior and the gnarled roots a pathway down to the underworld. According to Maori tradition, the earlier the pohutukawa blossoms, the longer and hotter the summer to come.

In Australia, "Christmas tree" can mean something very different than the noble evergreen we usually picture. It's actually the name of *Nuytsia floribunda*, a mistletoe that grows in southwestern Australia, blooming with bright orange flowers during the summer. But just like the holiday from which it gets its name, there is a dark side below the surface. The Australian Christmas tree is believed to be the largest parasite in the world, with roots that spear into the roots of any other plants it can reach, stealing their sap. It's so indiscriminate that it has even been known to cut through underground wires and cables.

HIMMELI:
MERRY MOBILES

FINLAND

*S*pot one of these lovely, understated Christmas decorations, and you might think you've stepped into a luxury home design store. *Himmeli* are traditional Finnish mobiles—that is, delicate sculptures attached with strings and suspended from the ceiling. Reeds or pieces of straw are carefully arranged into geometric configurations and typically hung over the dinner table. The name comes from the Swedish word *himmel*, meaning heaven, and traditionally, the more and larger the *himmeli* that have been hung from the ceiling, the bigger the household farm's crop would be expected to be in the coming year. Swedes also make these decorations, as do people in Poland, Lithuania, Belarus, and Russia.

These geometric mobiles have gone global in recent years as Scandinavian *hygge* design has become trendy. One can find how to construct one's own *himmeli* using traditional natural straw, modern plastic straws, or even thin brass tubes. The most basic design, which looks like a pair of pyramids attached at the base, can be constructed by threading any of these materials, three at a time, onto lengths of twine or string and creating a series of triangles. If one feels like getting more elaborate, there are tutorials of increasing difficulty. Recently, it has become popular to use these Finnish Christmas decorations all year round as plant hangers.

PAVUCHKY:
CELEBRATORY SPIDERWEBS

UKRAINE

*V*isiting a home in Ukraine over Christmas, you might think you had stepped into a Halloween celebration. Christmas trees, or *yalyna*, here are often decorated with silver and gold cobwebs and tiny decorative spiders, looking something like a prop belonging in a sparkly haunted house. But instead of being creepy, these arachnids are meant to evoke hope and love and all the nice things we usually associate with the holidays.

The tradition is rooted in a heartwarming Ukrainian folktale about a poor widow whose children were excited when a Christmas tree sprang up outside their home. But the mother had no money to decorate it, so on Christmas Eve, the family went to bed weeping. That night, the spiders heard their sobbing and proceeded to cover the tree with delicate, glistening webs that delighted the family upon waking and seeing the artful work.

In honor of this, many Ukrainian families decorate their trees with silver and gold cobwebs made of paper or wire, dotted with little spiders, or *pavuchky*. Some families even refuse to remove any spiders from their homes in the weeks leading up to Christmas. Spiders and spiderwebs pop up in traditional songs, children's books, and folk art.

The story is embellished and expanded in numerous other

ways. Some versions say the webs actually turned into silver and gold, while others say they merely looked like precious metals, leaving the widow feeling rich come Christmas morning. Another take connects it to the nativity. As the Holy Family sought safety from Herod's soldiers, they are said to have hidden in a cave, and the kindly spiders helped camouflage them by covering the entrance with webs, leading the soldiers to pass it without a second thought.

So as you tidy up your house ahead of the big holiday party, you might consider leaving that cobweb in the corner alone.

While the Christmas tree has been a decorative feature in Ukrainian homes since it was introduced from Germany in the nineteenth century, the more significant addition to the home during the holidays is the *didukh*. This is a sheaf of wheat and other grains that not only reminds those celebrating of the bounty from the fields for the year, but is said to contain the spirits of the ancestors (it literally translates to "grandfather spirit"), who enter the home to join in the Christmas festivities.

DZIAD AND BABA:
A CHANDELIER OF WHEAT

POLAND

*I*f you walked into a Polish home on Christmas Eve and saw a sheaf of grain hanging from the ceiling, tops pointed down, it would not seem odd to your host if you asked, "Is that an old man or an old woman?" These bundles of wheat, created by tying the ends of the stalks together with a string to look something like a farmer's chandelier, are known in some villages as *dziad* ("old man") or *baba* ("old lady"). They are both made the same way and the gender is decided by the maker. These were popular decorations long before Christmas trees ever became standard—in fact, some homes would skip the wheat and hang the top part of a spruce tree, upside down, from the ceiling to get that chandelier appearance. And hanging the sheaves of wheat was not just for the rural areas; many homes in the city adopted the practice as well.

In other regions nearby, bundles of wheat or rye might be brought into the house and tucked behind holy pictures or nailed to a ceiling beam. Bunches of the grain might be shaped into crosses or stars known as *krzyże wigilijne* ("Christmas Eve crosses") or might be placed on the table during the Christmas Eve feast.

Dziad or *baba* might also make an appearance on New Year's Day, when it will be whacked with a stick so that grain will fall, while the householder repeats the verse "For your good luck, for your good health." It will then be strewn in the field to aid the next year's harvest. More recently, mixed nuts have replaced the wheat, but the New Year wishes remain.

Another traditional Polish ornament is the "porcupine ball" or "little hedgehog"—the nicknames of the spiky, star-shaped *jeżyk* that decorates many homes in Poland during the holiday season. Made up of paper circles rolled into dozens of points jutting out from the center, the *jeżyk* is fairly simple to construct, requiring only colored paper, scissors, and needle and thread. Or there are the *lancuszki* garland chains made from paper fans, folded birds made of colorful tissue paper, or stars and globes made from *oplatek* wafers (read more about these on page 208).

The handmade quality of these decorations, and the tradition of Polish families and communities gathering together, served as a way to reinforce community bonds following the devastations of the two World Wars. As proud Poles sought to reject the German influence in their holidays by making handmade decorations based on traditional Polish folk art, Christmas decorating became a national effort of its own. So give that spiky star a closer look next time you see one—it represents a deeper history than its looks might lead you to believe.

CHICHILAKI:
A SHAGGY CHRISTMAS TREE

GEORGIA

*T*his beloved Yuletide decoration in the country of Georgia, created from dried hazelnut or walnut tree branches, looks a bit like a Christmas tree if its evergreen boughs had gone blond and it was overdue for a haircut. In fact, the curly, thin shavings connected to the top of the branch, making up this faux conifer, are thought to resemble the beard of Saint Basil the Great—the Santa-like gift-bringing saint associated with Christmas in the Eastern Orthodox tradition (see page TK). The handmade trees sold at market stalls across the Guria and Samegrelo regions can vary in length from eight inches to ten feet. Georgians place them in their homes, decorated with simple ornaments, bows, or berries and small fruits. Georgians view the *chichilaki* as a tree of life, representing hope and faith.

The symbolic power of these trees has grown over time and they are particularly potent today, considering the adversity faced by Georgians, and their ability to celebrate Christmas, over the past century. During the Soviet rule of Georgia, lasting from 1921 to 1990, the *chichilaki* was banned, along with other ceremonies and practices viewed as explicitly religious and unacceptable under Communist rule.

The *chichilaki* also reflect the reverence the Georgian people hold for their natural surroundings. The country's citizens view their beautiful forests as sacred and would not dream of chopping down firs to stick in their living rooms for a couple of weeks. Even those who do not have an emotional connection to the country's pines have a good financial incentive to opt for a *chichilaki*: In 2011, Georgia's government began charging steep fines to anyone spotted chopping down or transporting a pine tree (approximately US$1,200) and ramped up its rangers' patrols of the forests. Using the dead, dried branches of harvested nut trees offers a far more sustainable solution.

The *chichilaki* typically goes up on January 7, the date of Georgian Orthodox Christmas, and remains a fixture of the holiday home until the Georgian Orthodox Epiphany on January 19. On this day, with the *chichilaki* having served its decorative mission, Georgians do not set it out onto the sidewalk or some designated drop-off point. They burn the thing. This is not just some speedy disposal strategy, but a ceremonial release of the previous year's troubles during the Feast of the Epiphany, welcoming the promise of the New Year. In Samegrelo, some families bring home a *chichilaki* for each recently deceased family member.

Perhaps more central to the Georgian celebration of Christmas than the *chichilaki* is Alilo, the country's Christmas Day march. On January 7, thousands of Orthodox Christians take to the city streets in a religious procession. Priests wearing white robes and carrying banners lead parishioners and children decked out in colorful robes, holding icons such as suns and stars, while collecting food or presents for charity as they walk. Some marchers might dress up as characters from the nativity story or in traditional Georgian costumes. The donations are gathered at the church and then, following the religious service, distributed to orphanages, nursing homes, and others in need.

Alilo means "glory to God," and also refers to a traditional Georgian Christmas carol of the same name. The parade dates back to the fifth century as the faithful marched through the streets following Christmas Mass. Like other explicitly religious practices, it was banned during Soviet rule but has since come back stronger than ever. Anyone can join in the march or make a donation and sometimes the costumed children will break away from the parade, going house to house asking for gifts and donations.

BADNJAK:
A COMPLEX CHRISTMAS LOG

CROATIA AND SERBIA

*M*any European countries have a tradition of bringing a large Yule log into the home, providing warmth and a welcoming space during the depths of midwinter (see "Yule Log Night," on page 34). Sometimes this even extends to going out into the woods or backyard and chopping their own logs. But in Eastern Europe, the ceremony surrounding the Serbian *badnjak* requires a bit more from its practitioners.

The actual ceremony gets complex, with small variations from one region, or even one family, to another. Traditionally, it begins on the morning of Christmas Eve, at the crack of dawn, as the head of the household leads a group of male relatives into the woods to find a tree, sometimes kicking off the proceedings by ringing bells or firing guns. When they find a straight, young, healthy-looking oak (or, if that is not available, an elm, olive, or bay laurel), the fun begins.

The ideal specimen selected, the head of the household throws grain or corn at the tree and says something along the lines of "Good morning, Christmas!" After a brief ceremony that includes a prayer and kissing the bark, the leader chops the tree into a large log and the group carries it home (sometimes wearing gloves throughout the process, avoiding touching the now-holy object with their bare hands). Sometimes this extends to two or three young oaks for every house, with each male member of the family getting his own log, bringing the wood back home. Family members tie red silk and gold wire—and in some regions, a man's shirt—around the trunk, decorating it with leaves and flowers, and prepare it to be brought inside as twilight arrives. Lit candles are posted on either side of the door and as the head of the household crosses the threshold with the first log, greeting the family, another household member tosses corn on him and the log is set by the fire and sprinkled again with corn—or wine—as the father says, "Goodly be thy birth!" The fire is said to symbolize the one the shepherds, according to Serbian folk tradition, built in the cave where Jesus was born.

Straw may be spread across the floor just before or after the *badnjak* is brought inside, giving a manger-like feel to the home, sometimes with family members imitating a hen and her chicks as it is done. The straw might also be placed under the dinner table.

The family members pray over the log and sometimes set a bowl of corn or unleavened bread upon it as a way of wishing that the year ahead be one of abundance and fertile land. On Christmas Day, it is set on the fire and burns throughout the day.

Of course, traditions evolve over time. Nowadays, most Serbs use a store-bought *badnjak*, or the ceremony is conducted in the public square. The local church or town leaders organize the consecration and lighting of the *badnjak* (or oak twigs or saplings meant to represent the *badnjak*) in the churchyard or some other gathering space.

Another Serbian tradition connected with the burning of the *badnjak* is the Christmas Day arrival of the *polaznik*, the first visitor to enter the home. This person is thought to be a bringer of fortune, happiness, and other good things for the year ahead, so families will often arrange for a designated *polaznik* in order to ensure it is someone likely to bring blessings to the home. As with the *badnjak*, there are a number of rites to be observed.

The designated first person arrives early in the morning, carrying corn. They will shake out the corn on the threshold of the house and say, "Christ is born." A member of the house will sprinkle them with corn in return and answer, "He is born indeed." The *polaznik* will then go to the fire and strike the *badnjak*, burning in the fireplace, with a poker, wishing their hosts good fortune as plentiful as the sparks flying from the log.

A similar tradition can be found in Scotland and England. Known as "first-footing," it usually takes place on January 1, as opposed to Christmas Day in Serbia.

Chapter 7

FIERCE COMPETITIONS

LEISURELY PASTIMES

Christmas is a time of reflection and reverence, to be sure. But it is also a time to cut loose and have fun. Games are a key part of holiday celebrations throughout the world, whether in the form of a nationwide lottery where millions of dollars are on the line, or a playful poetry battle where the only prize is bragging rights. A friendly competition adds to the excitement of the holidays, and different countries have found very different ways to do just that.

NIGHT OF THE RADISHES: ELABORATE SCULPTURES MADE OF ROOT VEGETABLES

OAXACA, MEXICO

*A*nyone who has struggled to create a jack-o'-lantern will be mightily impressed by the carvers in the city of Oaxaca, Mexico. For most of the year, they practice their craft on wood, but when it comes time for La Noche de Rábanos, they turn to a very different medium: radishes. The root vegetable serves as the canvas for detailed characters and elaborate nativity scenes. Most of the carved tubers feature religious themes, of course, but some display scenes of daily life, famous people, Oaxacan legends, and even monsters. Oversize radishes, which grow to five pounds and heavier, are preferred; a salad radish is not ideal for creating characters that are about the size of a typical action figure, let alone the barns, buildings, and creatures that can reach several feet in size.

Radishes are not native to Mexico; the Spanish brought them over in colonial times, and during the annual Christmas market, to attract customers, a few radish growers began carving increasingly elaborate designs, finding that the vegetable's firm texture stood up well to sculpting. In 1897, the mayor of Oaxaca launched an official competition, and La Noche de Rábanos ("the Night of the Radishes") has been an annual tradition, held on December 23, ever since.

These days, there is a special garden where competitors can plant their radishes, leaving them in the ground for much longer than would normally be expected, to better allow them to grow to a massive size. A few days before the official competition, carvers harvest their vegetables and get to carving (any earlier and the radishes will have gone bad by competition day). While carvers may have an idea in mind for the scene they would like to create, sometimes the unique shape of a particular radish—a bump that could serve as a camel's back, a crease that could be part of a robe—will serve as inspiration.

The day of the event, the carvers set out their sculptures in the historic Zócalo plaza, and by late afternoon, lines of onlookers have formed around the block. By 9 p.m., the winners of the various categories are announced, with each receiving a cash prize (the grand prize winner can take home more than US$1,000), and a full-blown party kicks in with music, fireworks, and light shows throughout the square. But those artists who failed to earn a prize can still feel like winners: Most works are purchased by attendees to take home and use as a centerpiece for Christmas dinner.

SINTERKLAASGEDICHT: ROASTING THE ONES YOU LOVE WITH POETRY

NETHERLANDS

*W*hile children can expect to receive gifts and goodies as part of the Saint Nicholas's Day celebrations, adults in the Netherlands have found their own personalized gifts to share with friends and family as they gather for the feast: *sinterklaasgedichten*, or "Saint Nicholas poems."

A guest will write a poem specifically for another guest, reading it aloud as the other person unwraps a gift. Such personalized lines of verse probably sound like sweet gestures, and in many cases *sinterklaasgedichten* are wishes for health and good fortune. But more often, these poems are used to tease friends and family members, bringing up embarrassing memories or highlighting their less-flattering characteristics. It is the perfect opportunity to needle that cousin about all the baby photos they post on Facebook or bring up the way your brother chews his food with his mouth open.

A *sinterklaasgedicht* usually follows a simple format of rhyming couplets, running about a dozen lines and written from the perspective of Saint Nicholas himself, commenting on the naughty and nice things about the person and hinting at the gift they received, signed, "From Sinterklaas." While it is expected that the gift giver write the poem themselves, there are ready-written poems or even poem-writing services available for the less poetically inclined.

The poem is read as the subject takes part in another Saint Nicholas's Day tradition known as *surprise*. That's the term applied to the novelty gifts exchanged at the gathering, in which the gift itself is far less important than the way it is wrapped: A gray plastic bag could be done up to look like an elephant or a small item could be wrapped in layers and layers of yarn. The surprises often present obstacles or new challenges: A small gift could be frozen in a block of ice, or an elaborately wrapped box could contain just a slip of paper with a clue about where the "real" gift is hidden. All the festivities can take hours and the real rewards tend to be in expressing one's creativity and teasing appreciation for friends and family.

HOLY INNOCENTS' DAY PRANKS:
APRIL FOOLS IN DECEMBER

SPAIN, PHILIPPINES, AND LATIN AMERICA

*T*he Christmas season is a time of generosity, but if a friend asks you for some cash on December 28, you might think twice about offering the loan, particularly if you are in Spain, the Philippines, or a number of other countries that celebrate that date as Holy Innocents' Day.

The day is meant to honor a solemn subject—the Massacre of the Innocents, related in the Gospel of Matthew, when King Herod learned of the birth of Jesus and ordered the execution of all male children two years and younger in the general region of Bethlehem. Estimates of the number of victims range as high as more than 100,000, though many scholars consider the tale merely myth.

But rather than gravely paying tribute to these lost lives, many in Spanish-speaking countries recognize Holy Innocents' Day by playing pranks on one another. This can include putting salt in the sugar bowl, sticking paper dolls (*llufas*) on the backs of unwitting friends, ringing neighbors' doorbells and running away, or borrowing money with no intention of paying it back (hence the warning about loaning out cash to friends on December 28).

It might seem odd to celebrate in this way, but the tradition is said to be rooted in the "trick" the Wise Men pulled on King Herod by returning from Bethlehem along a different route than they had come, outwitting the king who wanted to find out from them the Christ child's location to kill him. Others say the pranks honor the deceptions parents would employ to protect their infants from the king's killers. Whatever the purpose, it usually means a lot of fun.

The Catholic Feast of the Holy Innocents is a serious reminder of the massacre, but the idea of an "Innocents' Day" has come to also refer to a childlike love of pranks in some parts of the world. When someone is accused of pulling a prank, they are likely to proclaim themselves "*¡Inocente, inocente!*" The fact that the holiday was often combined with the pagan Feast of Fools and raucous New Year's celebrations made it more naturally a time of fun than sorrow—except for those who loaned their friends money.

GANNA: HOLIDAY HOCKEY

ETHIOPIA

*A*lthough Ethiopia may not come to mind as a major hub of Christmas celebration, people there have actually been practicing Christianity at least as far back as the fourth century. Christians still make up a majority of the population, and while one is unlikely to come across Santa Claus or a Christmas tree there, those practicing the religion have developed many unique traditions. The Ethiopian Orthodox Tewahedo Church follows the Julian calendar, so Christmas, or Ganna (also spelled Genna), is celebrated on January 7. For the most part, the Ganna season is a deeply religious celebration, beginning with a forty-day fast and prayer vigils, leading up to a candle-lit procession to Mass, which can take up to three hours, standing the whole time (pews are not the norm in Ethiopian churches).

But in addition to the religious observance, Ethiopian Christians make plenty of time for fun, with dancing, feasting on *doro wat* (chicken stew), and playing games intermingled with the ceremonies. Perhaps the most beloved game is a kind of combination of soccer and hockey so linked with the holiday that it is called *ganna* as well. On the afternoon of Christmas Eve, all the men of the village go to a field or market square. The ball (a rounded piece of wood called a *srur* for the boys, a circular object wrapped in a strip of leather, called a *tsng*, for men) is set in the center of the makeshift field, and each player touches it with a long, curved stick and says a brief prayer that asks God to provide for the player through the rainy season.

The players are divided into two teams, divvied up by two of the party elders, or one village may compete against another. The two elders walk to the center of the field and strike the ground with their sticks twice, then strike their sticks against one another before each going for the ball. The game is now on and the members of each team fight furiously to get the ball into the other's goal (usually just a tree or other natural marker). They hit it across the field, or use their feet to scoop the ball into their hand, toss it in the air, and strike it with their stick like a baseball. Daring players might try to snatch away the ball as their opponent is about to hit it, which has led to serious hand injuries on a number of occasions. Each time a player scores a goal, the teams switch sides. There aren't any formal positions or many rules besides that players need to keep the ball on their right side.

It usually lasts until dusk, when it gets tough to make out the ball in the darkness and hunger for some Christmas feasting sets in. The team with the most goals wins bragging rights—until next Christmas.

The most involved holiday ceremonies of the Ethiopian Church celebrate Epiphany. On January 19, following the Gregorian calendar, *Timkat* ("Baptism") is celebrated with a procession led by a priest carrying a replica of the Ark of the Covenant *(tabot)*. He takes it to a nearby lake or river, and, early morning the next day, following a night of dancing and feasting, the priest submerges a cross in the water, blessing it. Worshipers then wash themselves in the water, receiving the blessing.

SURVAKANE:
A LUCKY CHRISTMAS SWAT

BULGARIA

*M*any Christmas traditions play on the idea of reversals: bosses being deferential to their workers, the poor receiving tributes from the rich, and children getting a chance to call the shots instead of their parents. The Bulgarian custom of *survakane* embodies just this sort of "kids rule" ethos, giving the children of the family a chance to mete out some playful corporal punishment—all in the name of passing along good luck for the year to come.

The most important step is creating the *survachka*, using a curled tree branch from a cornel (or dogwood) tree, whose branches are bent to its side, giving it a shape resembling the Slavic Cyrillic letter Ф. The stick is then decorated with strings of popcorn and coins, colored thread, dried fruits, nuts, foil and more. Every region in Bulgaria has its own particular way of decorating the *survachka*—in the north, seeds and bread are more popular, while coins are the go-to ornament in the south.

The youngest member of the family—traditionally a boy, but nowadays girls as well—takes the *survachka* and lightly lashes the backs of their family members, beginning with the oldest person and making their way to the youngest and even the family pets and livestock. As the child goes, they sing a song or recite a poem full of good wishes for the New Year, expressing hopes of prosperity and good health for each person. This ritual is believed to provide these good things to each individual and to the household generally, delivering the Bulgarian proverb of "New year, new luck." Anyone touched by the *survachka* will have the evil of the old year cleansed away and be ready for a year full of wealth, health, and fertility. And as a show of gratitude for this good-luck beating, the one wielding the *survachka* is often rewarded with treats or money from their family members.

Neighboring Romania has its own take on this tradition in the *sorcova*, a small bundle of twigs from fruit trees left in water to sprout. Nowadays, most people use artificial flowers, which might be a good thing, since the children of the house get to take the *sorcova* and go around whacking the adults with it on New Year's Day.

A popular recitation goes:
Happy, fertile year,
red apples in the garden,
a house, full with silk.
Live healthier next year,
next year and so forth.

AGUINALDOS: HOLIDAY BATTLE FOR POINTS

COLOMBIA

*T*he Spanish word *aguinaldo*, meaning "gift" or "bonus," sig-
nifies a number of things in Spanish-speaking countries
during the Christmas season. In most places, it refers to mone-
tary Christmas bonuses that employers are required to pay their
workers. In others, it is a song similar to a Christmas carol. But in
Colombia, Christmas *aguinaldos* are simple games played by children or flirty young couples, in which points (or "bonuses") are
earned for those who outmaneuver their competitors.

A few classic *aguinaldos*:

***Tres Pies* ("Three Feet"):** Someone tries to slip one foot in between
another partygoer's feet without being noticed, earning a point
when they do.

***Si o No* ("Yes or No"):** A player must go an entire evening with-
out saying "yes," while his partner is prohibited from saying "no,"
or both players must avoid using both words. Whatever the rules,
each player will get creative finding ways to get the other to say the
taboo word.

***Pajita en Boca* ("Straw in Mouth"):** When someone says the words
"*pajita en boca*," their partner will have to put a straw (or candy or
some other simple object) in their mouth or lose points. A player
can strike an agreement with their competitor that the straw can

be removed during meals—but must return immediately once dessert is finished.

***Beso Robado* ("Stolen Kiss"):** Played between couples, this game demands that one partner avoid being kissed by the other. If one partner sneaks a kiss, they get a point.

***Preguntar y No Responder* ("Ask and Not Answer"):** Similar to *Sí o No*, this game requires that a player not answer any question their competitor asks of them, finding clever ways to express themselves that does not involve giving an answer to a question.

There may be a betting component to *aguinaldos*, with players wagering a treat or meal or some other reward for the winner, or penalty for the loser—though usually earning more points than the other person is incentive enough for some fierce holiday contests.

Colombians celebrate Novenas, a nine day series of gatherings in private homes for prayer, singing, and partying very similar to *las posadas*, so some of these challenges might last for a week or more. On Christmas Eve, however, the games end and everyone tallies up their scores—and usually even those with the lowest scores still get gifts.

---✦---

LOTERÍA DE NAVIDAD:
VERY GENEROUS CHRISTMAS PRESENTS

SPAIN

*E*ach year, on the evening of December 22, a hush falls upon towns all across Spain and the traffic all but vanishes from the streets. It is not due to some reverent pre-Christmas church ritual, but the fact that most of those in Spain are gathered around their televisions, waiting to hear the winning numbers for El Gordo. Translated to "the fat one," that is the name for the prize of Spain's biggest annual lottery drawing, formerly known as Sorteo Extraordinario de Navidad, but most people simply call it Lotería de Navidad—the Spanish Christmas lottery. It is the second-longest-running lottery in the world, started in 1763, and has taken place on December 22 every year since 1812 (even continuing through the Spanish Civil War). Nearly 75 percent of adults in Spain take part in some form or another, with the average person spending 55 euros (about $58.96) on tickets in 2016.

The prizes, of course, are substantial, as the government takes only a 30 percent cut of the Lotería de Navidad. In 2018, the prize money totaled 2.38 billion euros (more than US$2.5 billion), with a top prize of 680 million euros (around US$754 million). But with so many people participating, the prize system has gotten complicated. The same lottery number appears on multiple tickets and a single ticket costs 200 euro (US$220), so people usually form groups or buy in quantities of one-tenth of a ticket (*un décimo*). In 2018, a total of 170 million *décimos* were up for sale.

This design means that the prize an individual actually receives is not that jaw-droppingly large—a top-winning ticket nets just 400,000 euros (US$443,620), and that's usually divided up further depending how many bought into that specific ticket—but this also means that many of the winners may be from the same area.

As might be expected, there is quite a celebration that goes along with drawing the winners. The event is televised, with students of San Ildefonso School in Madrid selecting the winning numbers and singing them out loud. While only one ticket wins El Gordo, all ticket buyers have about a 10 percent chance of winning their money back. However, people who do win often turn right around and buy a ticket for Lotería del Niño, the lottery held for the Epiphany on January 6.

Another game of chance popular in Spain during the holidays is the Urn of Fate. Slips of paper with the name of each guest at a party are tossed into an urn or bowl, from which pairs of names are drawn. It is said fate has determined each of these duos are to become good friends—or perhaps romantic partners—in the year ahead.

CHRISTMAS CRACKERS: EXPLOSIVE TREATS

ENGLAND

*T*he United Kingdom likes to celebrate Christmas with a bang—using the party favors known as Christmas crackers. These party gifts, made of a tube covered in bright colored paper, twisted at either end like a giant piece of wrapped candy, are passed out over the Yuletide meal. Guests are paired off, with each taking a side and giving it a good yank. The cracker splits with an audible pop, revealing a small toy, paper hat, plastic jewelry, riddle, or some other little gift. Like a wishbone, the cracker splits unevenly, and the person with the larger end claims the prize.

While these crackers rarely hold candy, they were originally invented by a candy maker. Tom Smith, the owner of a London sweet shop, is credited with inventing the Christmas cracker in the late 1840s. During a visit to Paris he encountered a French bonbon, a sugar-almond confection wrapped in tissue paper with a twist on either side. According to the candy man, while sitting by the fire one evening, as the log in the fireplace emitted a loud pop, a candy-colored lightbulb went off above his head. He conceived of how he could incorporate that element of pleasant surprise into a French-style bonbon by adding a small explosive mechanism to the wrapper, which he promptly patented.

Smith's original concept, and his idea to connect it with Christmas, has proven remarkably durable. The product has been modified over the years, with writers commissioned to compose topical notes, themed crackers (bachelor editions featuring false teeth and wedding rings, Millionaire's Crackers containing a piece of actual gold) and brands such as Sephora and Godiva getting in on the cracking-good fun.

These have become a mainstay of holiday celebrations in England and its commonwealth nations such as Ireland, Australia, Canada, and New Zealand. However, anyone considering taking them out of the country should be advised that many airlines now prohibit bringing them on board.

The world's longest Christmas cracker stretched to 207 feet, with a thirteen-foot width. Created by students and parents at the Ley Hill School and Pre-School, Chesham, Buckinghamshire, UK, it was unveiled on December 20, 2001. It contained an eight-foot hat, a bunch of balloons, and, of course, a joke.

Chapter 8

SAVORY
and
SATISFYING
HOLIDAY DISHES

For many, the Christmas feast is the highlight of the season. The flavor or smell of a particular dish can evoke stronger holiday feelings than even the most impressively decorated tree. But what constitutes a "Christmas meal" is very different in different cultures. For some it's a pig roast, for others, jellied whitefish; and in some parts of the world, a lengthy fast is the way to recognize the season.

☀
TWELVE-DISH SUPPER:
A MEAT-FREE FEAST

EASTERN AND CENTRAL EUROPE

*P*oland, Lithuania, Ukraine, Belarus, and Russia all share the tradition of a Christmas Eve supper made up of no less than twelve dishes. The names of the celebration and the dishes served vary by country, but in every region, the quantity of dishes is large and none of the ingredients include meat.

In Poland, Wigilia usually begins with the breaking of the *oplatek* wafer (see page 208) and a beet soup (aka red borscht), served with tiny dumplings stuffed with mushroom and onion. In Ukraine, Sviata Vecheria (Holy Supper) is not complete without sipping some *uzvar*, a sweet drink made from dried fruits and berries, and digging into a bowl of *kutya*, a dish of husked whole wheat grains sweetened with honey and raisins. In Lithuania, dinner on Christmas Eve, Kūčios, includes biscuits baked from unleavened dough, served only once a year and usually enjoyed with poppy-seed milk. But a number of dishes can be expected to appear on tables throughout the region, such as herring, carp, stuffed cabbage, sauerkraut, and pierogi dumplings.

The twelve dishes symbolize the twelve months of the year or the twelve apostles. While ready-made dishes have proliferated in stores and restaurants, it remains preferable to families to prepare the traditional recipes themselves.

When the first star can be seen in the sky, blessings are said and the meal can commence, usually enjoyed by candlelight. In some of these countries, an extra seat and place setting are put at the dinner table as an invitation to any spirits of departed family members, or members of the Holy Family, to join. Families may also place straw on or underneath the table as a reminder of Christ's birth in the stable, and a sheaf of wheat is often set in the corner as a symbol of fertility.

The Christmas Eve meal in Ukraine typically includes *kolach*, a braided bread in the shape of a ring that serves as a symbol of prosperity for the year to come. At the Christmas Eve dinner, it may be served stacked, with a candle in the center. Each member of the family cuts a piece, dips it in honey and salt, and greets the others with "*Khrystos razhdayetsya*" ("Christ is born").

LECHÓN DE NOCHEBUENA: A WHOLE HOG FOR THE HOLIDAYS

SPAIN, PHILIPPINES, AND LATIN AMERICA

*T*he Spanish word for Christmas Eve is Nochebuena or Noche Buena, literally "the good night" or "night of good tidings." For many Spanish-speaking countries and the Philippines, which was once colonized by Spain, it is the time for the biggest feast of the year, commemorating the joyous night when the Virgin Mary gave birth to the Christ child. The guest of honor is usually a whole roasted suckling pig. *Lechón* is the common centerpiece, but every country does things a little bit differently, and the pig's massive size usually means that popping it into the oven is not really an option.

For example, in Cuba, the Christmas pig is placed whole into a *caja china*, a roasting box of plywood lined with aluminum foil atop which hot coals are placed. Puerto Ricans usually season their *lechón asado* with oregano and garlic, mount it on a spit, and start cooking it up in the early hours of the morning, ensuring the party can start by the time the sun comes up. In the Philippines, where the dish originated, there are two schools of thought on the best way to prepare the pig: Cebu *lechón*, in which the pig belly is stuffed with herbs and roasted over coconut-husk charcoal, or Manila *lechón*, in which it is stuffed with salt and pepper and roasted over wood charcoal.

Romania has its own pig-focused holiday tradition in Ignat, Saint Ignatius Day. On December 20, a pig is slaughtered and its bristles singed with burning straw and washed. The head of the family may then make the sign of the cross on the porcine head, and the beast will then be roasted and feasted upon.

LUTEFISK:
AN OFFENSIVELY
DELIGHTFUL CHRISTMAS FISH

NORWAY AND THE MIDWESTERN UNITED STATES

*J*n Norway, Christmas Eve is the most important day of the Yuletide season, so that's when *joulupöytä*, or the Yule Table, is set. A Christmas ham is typically the main dish, but it is not the most noteworthy. That honor would probably go to lutefisk, a traditional Nordic fish dish whose preparation process is not the most appetizing. First, dried whitefish—usually cod—is soaked in a solution of water and lye (yes, the caustic chemical most associated with cleaning drains). The alkaline solution breaks down the protein in the fish and gives it a shining gloss, leaving it in a near-translucent, jellied state after several days of soaking. After being carefully washed and soaked in fresh water, it is ready to cook. In Norway, it is generally served with bacon, goat cheese, mustard sauce, or syrup, with boiled potatoes on the side.

In addition to the lengthy preparation required, lutefisk is notably delicate, easily breaking apart if not handled properly. It's also earned a reputation for giving off a pungent, fishy aroma that has inspired a popular parody in the United States of "O Tannenbaum."

For all these reasons, the dish fell out of favor during the second half of the twentieth century. But it has enjoyed something of a renaissance with reports of lutefisk consumption slowly increasing, primarily in the northern parts of Norway. Nonetheless, far more lutefisk is consumed in the United States by Scandinavian Americans than in Europe by Northern Europeans. Madison, Minnesota, is the self-proclaimed "lutefisk capital of the United States," where Scandinavian Americans gather for lutefisk feasts, enjoying the flaky fish with sides of mustard or cream sauce, the aroma of the ocean reminding them of Christmas in their motherland.

So, checking the scoreboard: Lutefisk has a bad smell and slimy texture, is difficult to prepare, and a key ingredient is lye. No wonder a popular T-shirt at Scandinavian gift shops reads TRY LUTEFISK AT YOUR OWN LUTE-RISK.

TOURTIÈRE:
MEAT PIE FOR THE HOLIDAYS

QUÉBEC, CANADA

*D*uring the chilly Christmas season in Québec, the cozy aromas of nutmeg, cloves, allspice. and cinnamon fill the homes of many a French Canadian household. It comes with the preparation of *tourtière*, a spiced meat pie packed with flavor—as well as hearty portions of pork or beef, potatoes, and onions—all encased in a flaky pastry. It is a staple of Réveillon, the traditional Québécois Christmas Eve dinner.

The dish's origin is debated, with some claiming it was imported from France as immigrants arrived to the province in the mid-seventeenth century. Others maintain a more nationalistic view—that the particular combination of spices and ingredients is uniquely Québécois, but that early versions of the dish were more likely to contain game birds than today's pork. As immigrants from Québec moved south, the dish has also found its way to the New England region of the United States, where families in Maine, Rhode Island, and Vermont cook it up. Regions, and individual families, differ in their approach to the pie, with some using veal, salmon, or rabbit, or using ground meat instead of cubed. Some eat it with maple syrup, others with cranberry preserves or even ketchup.

The name comes from the dish in which the pie is baked, also called a *tourtière*. The tradition used to be that *tourtière* would be served after midnight Mass or at the stroke of midnight on New Year's Eve, but now the dish is just as likely to grace tables a little earlier in the evening.

HALLACAS:
STUFFED CORNMEAL TURNOVERS

VENEZUELA

*A*s Venezuelan families gather on Nochebuena, feasting before they head to midnight Mass, a key part of the meal will be *hallacas*: cornmeal-dough pockets wrapped in plantain leaves and tied with string, like a delicious holiday gift waiting to be unwrapped. They are similar to the more familiar tamales, but these are packed with a mix of ingredients that might strike the uninitiated as a bit surprising: In addition to ground beef, chicken, or pork, the eater will encounter raisins, capers, olives, and maybe even hard-boiled egg, almonds, or whatever else is in the pantry.

The *hallacas* are usually prepared in a huge batch in several stages that can take an entire weekend. A huge pot of *guiso*, or stew, is made with meat, peppers, onion, and other ingredients like leeks, capers, and annatto seeds, and is left overnight in the fridge so the flavors can intermingle. The next day, extended family and friends gather around a long table or along the kitchen counter in an assembly line of holiday flavor.

One person sets a banana leaf on the table and flattens it. The next person adds a ball of dough made from ground corn, annatto grains, and pork fat and spreads it on top in a circular motion. A dollop of *guiso* is added, then strips of pepper and onion, a few raisins, a couple of chickpeas and capers, and whatever other ingredients appeal to the family. The next person folds the leaf, ensuring the whole thing is completely sealed. It is then tied with yarn both vertically and horizontally and tossed into a boiling pot for ninety minutes or so before being removed to cool. The cooks repeat this process a few dozen times (or a few hundred, depending on the size of the holiday party) to ensure they are well stocked for Nochebuena. If a family makes too many, that is fine, too—*hallacas* can keep for weeks, and extras can be frozen to enjoy months later.

The everything-but-the-kitchen-sink list of ingredients is said to have originated from slaves pulling together scraps from Spanish colonialists. It fits the complex influences of the country, bringing in elements of Spain, Latin America, and the Caribbean into a richly appetizing stew. But as good as it tastes, it is the preparation of these pouches of holiday flavor that really captures the region's Christmas spirit.

IL CAPITONE:
FRIED EEL FESTIVITIES

SOUTHERN ITALY

*H*oliday dining in Italy is as diverse and wide-ranging as one would expect in one of the world's culinary capitals. But one dish closely associated with Christmas, particularly in Naples and southern Italy, is eel. The main feast in Italy is *cenone* ("big supper") served on Christmas Eve, which often lasts hours (understandable, considering it traditionally follows a twenty-four-hour fast) before diners enjoy a postdinner espresso and head to midnight Mass. In Catholic tradition, the meal is meatless, with seafood such as calamari and *baccalà* (codfish) making up the bulk of the dishes, along with plenty of salads, breads, and pasta. The centerpiece is the *capitone*, a large female eel, fried (or sometimes steamed or roasted) and dished out with a variety of sauces or herbs.

The eels are typically sold live at the market, and selecting the perfect one is a key responsibility of the person preparing the feast. Considering that virtually every Italian family is facing the same demand, it can lead to a rush on the seafood vendors, who sell thousands of pounds of the fish, with lines snaking around the stalls, not unlike the eels themselves.

With seafood at the center of the Italian holiday feast, a tradition that is reputed to have begun in southern Italy but has truly taken off among Italian Americans in the United States is Festa dei Sette Pesci, or the Feast of the Seven Fishes.

Just as it sounds, this holiday banquet consists of at least seven fish dishes, running the gamut from trout dip to lobster and linguine to *cioppino* fisherman's stew. There are few hard-and fast rules about which dishes to prepare, or even the number of courses—while the number in the name is said to honor the seven Catholic sacraments, it is not unusual to extend it to twelve seafood dishes, one for each of Jesus's disciples. But seafood must be served, with pasta, salads, and bread on the side, and generous amounts of wine, finished off with some Italian cookies or *panettone* fruit cake.

FORTY-THREE-DAY FAST:
A MONTH AND A HALF WITHOUT MEAT

*M*ost Egyptian Christians are part of the Coptic Orthodox Church, a segment of the faith that has its own pope and Christmas traditions. Like other Orthodox sects, they celebrate Christmas at the end of the first week of January. But for forty-three days before that, Coptic Christians eat a vegan diet—no animal products of any kind, including dairy and eggs.

It is part of the Fast of the Nativity, and while this may seem like a long time to go without meat, Coptic Christians fast up to 210 days out of the year, including 55 days during the Great Fast over Lent and 15 days for Virgin Mary, plus 3 days for the Fast of Nineveh, in honor of the tale of Jonah and the whale. The belief is that in the Garden of Eden, before Adam and Eve succumbed to temptation, humans did not eat any animal products. It was only sin—humanity's "carnal" nature—that made people desire meat.

Followers will typically break the fast on Christmas Day with *fata*, a rich stew of lamb, butter, garlic, and hunks of toasted bread. This will often be accompanied by sweet biscuits emblazoned with the sign of the cross.

Many Orthodox faiths practice a forty-day fast for Advent as a way to mirror Moses's forty-day fast before receiving the Ten Commandments, but Coptic Christians add on three extra days.

These three days are technically a separate fast, commemorating the tenth-century miracle when Saint Simon the Tanner helped move Cairo's Mokattam Mountain. After fasting for three days, Simon gave Coptic Pope Abraham God's instructions for shifting the mountain, a miracle that impressed the current caliph so much that he declared the Christian faith to be true.

The celebration of Coptic Christmas did not become a national holiday in Egypt until 2003, thanks to a presidential decree by Hosni Mubarak. Previously only Muslim holidays were considered national, as just about 10 percent of the country's citizens are Christian.

DOPP I GRYTA:
A FONDUE TO REMEMBER FAMINE

SWEDEN

The people of Sweden celebrate Christmas more extravagantly than most, which is clear to anyone who has had the chance to experience *julbord*. This holiday buffet is a spread of Scandinavian dishes fit for royalty: pickled herring and cured salmon, pickled vegetables, beet salad, meatballs, sausage, Christmas ham, and plenty of sweets and pastries to round it off. Plates are piled high and there is no shame in going back for seconds or thirds.

But amid the prep of all the cold meats, plentiful fish, and cookies, the *julbord* feasting will usually include a dish that is meant not only to taste delicious, but to acknowledge when food was not always so abundant.

On Christmas Eve, after the midday meal is cooked, the family and their guests gather around the table for a ritual called *dopp i gryta* ("dipping in the kettle" or "dip in the pot"). Each person picks up a piece of dark bread and dips it into cooking broth—the thickening juices of the traditional Christmas ham or a specially prepared pot made by simmering pork or corned beef served as part of lunch. The friends and family members wish one another a merry Christmas as they eat the bread, fondue style.

Dopp i gryta is an effective way to tide over appetites between lunch and the Christmas Eve dinner. But it also may be treated as an opportunity for a solemn remembrance of the less bountiful times of ancestors, when every bit of the Christmas ham was savored and stretched into as many meals as possible. However it is enjoyed, the practice has become such a key part of Swedish holiday traditions that it is not unusual for Christmas Eve to be referred to as *dopparedagen*, or "dipping day."

The Swedish Christmas feast often includes rice porridge in which a single almond has been hidden. But the person who finds the almond does not receive a gift—they are expected to provide a gift to the rest of the guests, in the form of a rhyme expressing their gratitude for the meal or striking some other seasonal note.

✳
MARBINDA:
SHARING THE COW

NORTH SUMATRA, INDONESIA

*I*ndonesia is a vast country, stretching across seventeen thousand islands and covering more than 700,000 square miles. So it makes sense that the Indonesian people also celebrate Christmas in a wide variety of ways. Though it is a Muslim-majority country, millions of Christians live there, not to mention non-Christians who just enjoy getting into the Christmas spirit. The Torajan people of South Sulawesi take part in a festival of dancing and handicrafts known as Lovely December. On Christmas Eve in the province of Maluku, ship sirens are sounded at the same time that church bells are rung, creating a celebratory cacophony.

But one of the most interesting celebrations of Natal (from the Portuguese word for "Christmas") on Indonesia takes place in the North Sumatra region, where the Batak people take part in a Christmas tradition that binds the community together—by killing a large animal. In the days and weeks leading up to Christmas, locals give money to a community pot. If they gather enough, they will buy a cow or buffalo. If the pot is not quite big enough for that, they may buy a pig. Then all come together on Christmas Day to slaughter the animal, splitting the meat up equally among those who contributed (*marbinda* translates "to distribute"). While it might not be something that many would think of doing on Christmas, it is a tradition meant to promote generosity and create a sense of community.

─※─
LITTLE FEAST:
BREAKING A LONG FAST

IRAN

*J*ran is a predominantly Muslim country, but there is a minority of Christians that includes Catholics, Protestants, evangelicals, Armenians, and Assyrians. As with Christians in other nations, Iranian Christmas celebrants decorate with nativity scenes. However, their own unique tradition is the Little Feast, a not-so-little assortment of Persian dishes like harissa (a chicken and barley stew), *dolmeh* (stuffed grape leaves), or *reeshaw aqle* (tripe soup). Dessert is a traditional dish called *kada* or *kadeh*, a sweet, buttery pastry.

This is a "Little Feast" not because of its size, but because the great feast occurs at Easter, celebrating the resurrection of Jesus as the most important event of the Christian year. Both feasts are preceded by a time of fasting—the Little and Great Fasts, respectively—where believers avoid meat, dairy, and eggs. This is similar to Lent, but Iranian Christians (and others who celebrate Advent with fasting) also practice it at Christmastime. The fasts are meant to cleanse the body and mind in preparation for the holy day. Families generally attend church on both Christmas Eve and the morning of Christmas Day, after which they return home and break the Little Fast in a big way.

JOLLOF RICE:
A ONE-POT STAPLE

WEST AFRICA

*A*lthough jollof rice is not only served on December 25, no Christmas dinner in this region would be complete without it. The deep-red dish mixes rice with tomatoes, onions, peppers, salt, and spices into a beloved and easy-to-make one-pot meal that is something like the cousin of Spain's paella or Louisiana's gumbo. Rice is a staple food in most West Africans' diet, and jollof rice is a chance to showcase the ingredient.

On Christmas, it may be presented a little more formally, shaped into mounds or topped with garnishes. But one wades into a heated debate when talking about the origin or proper way to make jollof rice. In Ghana, it tends to be made with basmati rice and beef or goat meat, then eaten with fried plantains or on its own. In Nigeria, it is more likely to be prepared with parboiled rice and stock cubes and may be served with seafood (though the exact combination of ingredients varies from place to place, and even family to family). The word *jollof* derives from the name of the Wolof kingdom—an ancient empire that stretched across modern-day Senegal, Gambia, and Mauritania. It is a dish meant to be shared, with the host family cooking up the ingredients in several large pots before serving in colorful bowls fit for a Christmas celebration.

KENTUCKY FOR CHRISTMAS:
A FITTING FEAST FOR
A WESTERN CELEBRATION

JAPAN

*I*f you put a red stocking cap on him, wouldn't Colonel Sanders look a lot like Santa Claus? As it happens, KFC is the go-to Christmas dinner in Japan, with millions of Japanese families heading to their nearest franchise to pick up a bucket of "Christmas Chicken." Christmas Eve is consistently the biggest sales day in Japan for the fast-food chain, with families ordering their buckets in advance or waiting in long lines for takeout. KFC offers special Christmas dinner packages and specialty chicken buckets, runs television commercials featuring families gathered around barrels of chicken, and even hires Santa-suited Colonel Sanderses to appear in front of restaurants.

Though accounts vary, the story goes that in the early 1970s, as KFC franchises had first begun opening in the country, a few American expats wandered into the first KFC restaurant, commenting that since Christmas turkey was near impossible to come by in the Land of the Rising Sun, fried chicken could be the next-best thing. The store's manager, Takeshi Okawara, saw an opportunity and began promoting his deep-fried offerings as a hearty holiday feast. KFC took the idea and ran with it, launching a national holiday campaign in 1974 that urged *Kurisumasu ni wa Kentakkii!* ("Kentucky for Christmas!"). It proved a hit, and the company continued the campaign year after year, inventing a new tradition in the process.

In a country where Christmas was more of a Western novelty (only about 1 percent of Japan's population is Christian), fried chicken made for an appropriate meal and it soon became one of the defining holiday traditions in the country, sold in limited-edition buckets and dinner packages complete with cake and wine. The manager who came up with the idea in the first place also did all right, moving up the ranks and serving as president and CEO of KFC Japan for almost two decades.

In addition to fried chicken, the other key ingredient of Christmas in Japan is romance. Young couples have turned December 25 into their own Valentine's Day, exchanging gifts with their sweethearts, going out for a fancy meal (generally a cut above KFC), and staying at a nice hotel for the night.

Chapter 9

CELEBRATORY
SWEETS

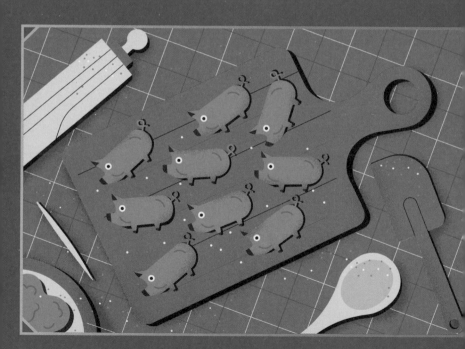

During the holidays, dessert is not restricted
to the end of a meal—sweets are ubiquitous:
in shops, set out for visiting friends and family,
and flooding the break room of seemingly
every office. Whether homemade, store bought,
or prepared with the family for the big feast,
Christmas sweets provide steady pleasures
throughout the season, and ones that are
as particular to a culture or country
as its own language.

ROSCÓN DE REYES:
A DESSERT HIDING A SECRET PRIZE

SPANI
SPAIN

*O*n the evening of Three Kings Day in Spanish-speaking countries, children leave out biscuits for the Magi and water or
hay for their camels. But those celebrating their gifts get to enjoy
a slightly tastier snack on January 6: the *roscón de reyes* or "ring of
the kings."

This large ring of sweet bread, baked in the Wise Men's honor,
is festooned with dried or candied fruit such as cherries, quince,
and figs, with a thin layer of icing on top. Its oval shape with the
colorful spots of fruit is meant to represent a bejeweled ring or
crown. The cake usually delivers a surprise—a small figurine of the
baby Jesus hidden in the cake to represent the clandestine escape
of the Holy Family from King Herod.

Whoever receives the piece with the figurine is considered
blessed and is expected to take the figurine to church on February
2, Candlemas, which celebrates the day Jesus presented himself t
the Temple of Jerusalem to be officially inducted into Judaism. In
this way, the person who receives the figurine (usually the adult
who prepared the cake arranges for that slice to go to one of the
children) is said to be helping Jesus along his life's path.

The tradition of a showstopping cake baked for Epiphany, usually hiding some object inside, appears in numerous cultures and countries, each with its own particular traditions and details. Among the most prominent examples:

GALETTE DES ROIS
(BELGIUM, NORTHERN FRANCE, AND QUÉBEC)

Flaky puff pastry surrounds a dense center of frangipane almond cream, or sometimes fruit or chocolate, into which a *fève* (fava bean) is baked. The person who gets the slice with the bean in it is "king for the day" and wears a gilded paper crown (bakeries in France will often include the crown with the cake). Some bakeries will bake these tarts into special shapes, such as cartoon characters or historical figures, while higher-end places will use a different trinket as the *fève* each year, making them collector's items.

TORTELL OR GÂTEAU DES ROIS OR
ROYAUME (SOUTHERN FRANCE)

This yeasted cake in the shape of a circle is decorated with candied fruit. Very similar in appearance to the *roscón de reyes*, this dessert traditionally contains two surprises: a dried field bean and a figurine of one of the Wise Men. Unlike with the *galette des rois*, the person who finds the king gets to wear a paper crown and be "king for the day," while the person who finds the bean has to pay for the cake.

BOLO-REI (PORTUGAL)

This has the ring shape of the *roscón de reyes*, and is usually filled with candied fruit and occasionally nuts. A coin is often hidden as the prize in addition to the fava bean, and whoever finds the bean must provide the cake the next year.

—⟋—

VASILOPITA (GREECE AND CYPRUS)

More likely to be enjoyed on New Year's Day than Epiphany, the *vasilopita* is round and flat, with almonds on top. It more closely resembles the French *galette* and includes a hidden coin or trinket that brings good luck.

—⟋—

BANITSA (BULGARIA)

Served on New Year's Eve as well as at other celebrations such as weddings and festivals, this version of the cake is made by wrapping sheets of phyllo dough around a filling of soft cheese, egg, and yogurt. It will contain trinkets inside such as small pieces of dogwood branch (associated with Christmas in Bulgaria; see *"Survakane"* on page TK) as well as foil-wrapped fortunes predicting all the good things the recipient can expect in the coming year.

—⟋—

KING CAKE (UNITED STATES GULF COAST)

It is said that the king cake tradition was brought to the southern United States in the early 1700s as part of the Epiphany celebration. But here it is eaten throughout the Carnival season, from Epiphany to Fat Tuesday, when it serves as a final indulgence before the constraints of Lent and one of the icons of Mardi Gras. The cake is closer to the Spanish-style *roscón de reyes*, though with a heavy layer of icing on top and glittery sprinkles in the Mardi Gras colors of green, gold, and purple (representing faith, power, and justice).

TWELFTH NIGHT CAKE (UNITED KINGDOM)

This was once a staple of Epiphany celebrations in the United Kingdom, baked with a bean on one side and a pea on the other. According to one 1920s etiquette book, "the man finding a bean in his slice is elected King; the lady finding a pea is his Queen" and the two are seated on thrones and given paper crowns, scepters, and "if possible, full regalia." Perhaps because of all the complications involved, this practice and the cake itself have fallen out of favor, and today one is more likely to find a fruitcake on tables in England during the Christmas season.

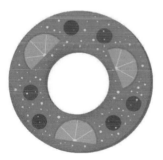

OPLATEK:
BREAKING THE WAFER

POLAND

*M*any Christmas feasts and treats, particularly in non-Anglo-Saxon countries, are known for their strong, robust flavors that celebrants associate with the winter holidays. However, the Polish *oplatek* is practically the opposite—a thin, near-flavorless wafer. Polish Catholics abstain from meat in the days before Christmas, and the Christmas Eve dinner generally includes fried fish, boiled potatoes, and pea soup. However, before this meal, some Polish and other Eastern European families hold a brief ceremony.

Traditionally, the father (as the male head of the household) picks up the *oplatek* wafer and offers words of hope for the new year and apology to his wife for any failings over the previous year. She then takes the *oplatek*, eats a small piece, and offers the same to her husband and then to the oldest relative in attendance, expressing her hope that all in attendance will be there again at the next Wigilia (Christmas Eve) dinner. The wafer is passed from person to person, each one (even the youngest children) breaking off and eating a piece and expressing their love for their family members in front of all the others. A common wish of good fortune one might hear: "Wishing you health, good luck, and great fortune, and after death, a crown in heaven."

Like the Christian sacrament of communion, the passing of the unleavened *oplatek* represents breaking bread, though the spiritual connection with God has been exchanged for the earthly connection with family. During World War II, when families were often separated, and continuing to this day, some families would mail pieces of the *oplatek* to their distant loved ones to show them that they're still part of this Christmas tradition.

In Polish households, when the table is set for Christmas dinner, families may put out one extra place setting in front of an empty chair. This is a symbolic act of hospitality meant to show that any guest who shows up at that family's door will have a place at the table. The practice is said to have come from the old Slavic pagan practice of "sweeping" an empty chair with your hand before sitting to clear away any spirits who may have gathered there. When Christianity came to Poland, this practice was adapted to commemorate family members who had passed away in the past year.

APPLES:
A HEALTHY HOLIDAY GIFT

CHINA

*C*hristmas is not a public holiday in China, and considering that Christians make up about 5 percent of the population, it is hardly the national event found in most Western nations. But that is not to say that the day goes by totally unrecognized, and in fact, its popularity has been growing, particularly with younger Chinese. But it tends to be thought of like Valentine's Day, as a time when couples can enjoy a romantic meal. Or young Chinese may acknowledge December 25 by shopping or dining with friends. However they celebrate, they tend to get each other one particular gift: an apple.

In China in December, shop windows have begun to fill up with brightly decorated apples. They may be wrapped in paper or ribbons, or they may have Christmas greetings printed right on the skin. Why apples? It is actually a bit of wordplay that got out of hand. The Chinese term for Christmas Eve, *píng'an yè* (平安夜) translates to "peaceful night." The word for apple is *píngguo* (苹果), which translates to "peaceful fruit" and sounds very similar to *píng'an yè*.

These apples are not sold like one would see in the produce aisle of a Western grocery store, but are instead individually wrapped in colorful paper or packaged in decorative boxes with *Merry*

Christmas stenciled on them (or, more often, symbols of romance such as hearts and lips, looking more like a simple valentine than a Christmas gift). These are then given out as a kind of an offering of "peace" for the year ahead. Taking the puns a step further, some more generous gift givers will provide their partners with Apple-brand devices or products.

The encroachment of Christmas has not been without controversy. In recent years, city and provincial authorities in some parts of the country have cracked down on "Western festivals," urging teachers to instead help strengthen their students' understanding of traditional Chinese culture and festivals.

But despite the Communist government, when it comes to spotting a market opportunity, China's fruit sellers are happy to play by the rules of supply and demand. For most of the year, you can buy a kilogram of apples in China for 6 to 8 yuan (about US$1.00). However, during the Christmas season, the price shoots up to 78 yuan (about US$12.18) per apple.

RISALAMANDE:
HOLIDAY RICE PUDDING

DENMARK

*P*rior to World War II, limited worldwide shipping meant that the Danish prized a particular ingredient: rice. Throughout the year, porridge would typically be made with water and a grain such as barley, oats, or rye. So during the holidays, when a family could afford to make pudding with rice, it was a special treat. Add vanilla, whipped cream, chopped almonds, and cinnamon (another previously limited resource), and you've got a very special, rather exclusive dish: *risalamande*.

After World War II, increased trade made rice much easier to import, and more affordable, so the dessert became increasingly popular—though it was still only really enjoyed during the holiday season. The name comes from an adaptation of a French expression for "rice with almonds," *riz á l'amande* (though there is little French about its origins). Typically, a family will make a huge batch of rice pudding at the beginning of the Christmas season and save some to whip into *risalamande* for Christmas. It is usually served cold with a dollop of cherry sauce on top. Often a whole almond will be hidden in the bowl of pudding—and the person who receives it wins a prize.

Another variety of rice pudding popular in Scandinavia is *julegrøt* (Yule porridge), also called *tomtegröt* in Sweden and *nissegrød* in Norway after the *tomte* or *nisse*, the mythical short and bearded "homestead man" who is said to watch over the farms of Sweden, Norway, and Denmark, caring for animals and keeping things tidy— demanding only respect and a bit of rice pudding in return. This pudding tends to be made with cinnamon and sugar, with an "eye" of butter in the middle (of which the *tomte* are said to be particularly fond).

MARZIPAN PIG:
SWEET SWINE

NORWAY AND GERMANY

*T*here's nothing lost in translation here; it's literally a small pig made out of marzipan—a combination of ground almonds, milk, and sugar, and a favorite Scandinavian sweet. Like the Danish, Norwegians eat rice pudding at Christmas, only their version is a hot dish called *risgrøt* or *risengrysnsgrøt*. They also hide an almond in the dish, and the person who finds it gets the marzipan pig, usually decorated with a bright red bow. In some homes, the winner may also receive the honor of passing out Christmas gifts.

Germans also give out marzipan pigs during the holidays. But they are more likely to distribute them as tokens of good luck for the New Year, and *Schwein gehabt*, or "having a pig," has come to mean having good luck in the region. It is particularly popular in the northern town of Lübeck, where a number of confectioners do brisk business in the sweet swine candies, including one that earned a Guinness World Record for largest marzipan pig by creating one weighing 2,215 pounds.

NOAH'S PUDDING:
THE OLDEST DESSERT IN THE WORLD

ARMENIA

A sweet porridge made with boiled wheat and naturally sweet ingredients such as cinnamon, fruit, and nuts, *anoush abour* ("sweet soup") is a staple of any Christmas feast in Armenia. It shares a lot with similar desserts, such as Ukraine's *kutya* and England's frumenty, as well as neighboring Turkey, where a similar dish is known as *ashure* and served during the first month of the Islamic calendar. But due to a legend based on the biblical character of Noah, the dish has also earned the nickname "the oldest dessert in the world."

The story goes that Noah was running low on food after forty days and forty nights of flooding, and all those animals and family members on the ark had to eat something. He asked his family to gather up whatever scraps they had, and they came back with—you guessed it—wheat, dried fruit, and nuts. Noah began cooking some *anoush abour*, and before he could finish, God put an end to the rain and directed Noah to Mount Ararat, where he could finally go ashore. That pudding was the last meal they all had to eat aboard the ark, and Armenians tell this story to go along with the dish to remind themselves to be thankful for God's goodness.

As with many Christmas specialties, every family seems to have its own take on the recipe, but the common elements are boiled grain, dried fruit, and nuts, sometimes set atop the porridge in a decorative pattern. Wheat berries and pearled barley are the most common grains called for, and apricots, golden raisins, and almonds are the most common accoutrements. The whole dish may be flavored with cinnamon, rosewater, orange flower water, honey…or nothing at all.

Noah's pudding has gained symbolic power outside of its native region. In England, the nonprofit Dialogue Society, founded by British Muslims of Turkish origin, encourages interactions between different cultures and religions by distributing bowls of the dessert. Not only do these events aim to encourage interactions between those of religions that recognize the figure of Noah—including Jews, Christians, and Muslims—but the sweet porridge itself serves as a model of harmony in diversity. "In Noah's Pudding, the mixing of different ingredients results in a delicious explosion of flavours," as the organization's pamphlet on its Noah's Pudding events reads. "So too, when diverse communities come together something good can come about from their interaction and conversation."

KULKULS:
SWEET COCONUT CURLS

INDIA

*T*hough we might associate holiday celebration in India with festivals such as Diwali, Holi, and Eid al-Fitr, this vast country is home to a sizable population of Christians, who celebrate Christmas with gusto, particularly in the cities of Goa and Mangaluru, where Catholicism is more widespread than in the rest of the country. A key part of the celebration is *kuswar*, a collection of Christmas sweets, which are prepared over a few busy days in the kitchen as the women of an extended family whip up such treats as cardamom macaroons, snowball-like *nankatais*, *newrio* (sweet dumplings stuffed with palm sugar and grated coconut), and *doce* (a goody made of chickpeas and coconut).

While the dozens of treats prepared vary depending on the region, a staple of any *kuswar* is *kulkuls*—sweet dough curls that can be eaten plain or after being rolled in sugar icing. They are made by dividing dough made of flour, egg, sugar, and coconut milk into marble-size bits, which are then pressed into rectangular shapes with a fork or comb, then rolled into small cylinders and deep fried, and finally set out and quickly gobbled up by visiting friends and family. They might also go by the names *kidyo* or *kidiyo*, which in Konkani, the official language of Goa, means "worms."

BÛCHE DE NOËL:
A YULE LOG MADE TO BE EATEN

FRANCE

*T*he Yule log is a key part of Christmas celebrations for many cultures, used to warm the home, bring holiday cheer, and burn away misfortunes from the year before. But in France and French-speaking regions, they actually eat the Yule log. Well, not the actual log, but a log-shaped cake known as a *bûche de Noël*, that's a popular addition to the huge feast over which many French Catholics gather following Midnight Mass. Known as *le réveillon* ("the awakening"), this spread can include fifteen courses or more—and the *bûche de Noël* usually makes an appearance. It is made from a flat sheet of sponge cake on which a buttercream or similar filling is spread. The cake is then rolled into a cylinder and iced with chocolate, with bits of hardened chocolate added to resemble tree bark. Bakers can get creative by adding details such as spun-sugar spiderwebs, pistachio moss, or meringue mushrooms.

Versions of the cake may date as far back as the 1600s, but it was Paris bakeries in the nineteenth century that popularized the modern version we know today. It has grown more popular in French households and internationally, providing an opportunity to be inventive with the decorations and create something that looks almost too good to eat.

CHIN CHIN:
DECEPTIVELY SIMPLE SWEETS

NIGERIA

A holiday celebration in West Africa usually includes a heaping pile of addictive *chin chin* sweets. Originating in Nigeria, these wheat flour treats have a simple flavor of nutmeg and lemon zest, and are so small and unassuming, it is too easy to pop them in your mouth one after another. Their addictiveness is largely due to the fact that they are fried (at the time the recipe was developed, ovens were not a standard appliance in most West African households), delivering a crispness that is hard to resist. There is some regional variation, with some sweeter, some more savory; some soft, some crunchy. But the key is that they be fried and small.

SZALONCUKOR:
A DECORATION AND A TREAT,
ALL IN ONE

HUNGARY

*A*lthough *szaloncukor* ("parlor candies") are a Hungarian sweet, they originated in France. A Lyonnaise candy maker began selling small chocolate-dipped sweets wrapped in colorful paper with quotes, riddles, or puns written on the inside. Later, German pastry chefs brought the idea for these confections into Hungary, where candy manufacturers began mass-producing them. The candies themselves may contain jelly (the most popular variation), coconut, marzipan, hazelnut, chestnut, or other fillings.

At the beginning of the Christmas season, Hungarian families tie these sweets on strings to the Christmas tree. As the season wears on, the wrappers "mysteriously" lose the candies inside, so the tree stays decorated as the children satisfy their taste for sweets.

COZONAC:
SWEET CHRISTMAS BREAD

ROMANIA AND MOLDOVA

*A*s a sweet, yeast-raised bread, the Romanian *cozonac* resembles the German *Stollen* and the Italian *panettone*. These fruit-filled Christmas breads have a common ancestor that may go back as far as ancient Egypt. The Egyptians sweetened bread with honey and added seeds. Then the Greeks borrowed the recipe and added yeast. The Romans added dried fruit and the tradition spread, along with their empire, all across Europe.

Today, the *cozonac* is an important part of a Romanian Christmas. The basic dough is more or less the same throughout the country—a mix of milk, flour, butter, sugar, and eggs—but fillings differ by region. Some add raisins and orange or lemon zest; others add walnuts or hazelnuts. Still others do not mix in the additions, but spread them across the flattened dough and then roll the dough up, producing a loaf with swirls of filling.

BLACK FRUITCAKE:
A BOOZY, TIME-INTENSIVE TREAT

TRINIDAD AND TOBAGO

*F*ruitcake gets a bad rap these days, but those who say they hate it are probably just not putting enough rum in it. Or enough time. Trinidad and Tobago's black fruitcake requires a lot of both: It starts with soaking prunes, raisins, and other fruits in a mixture of dark rum, cherry brandy, and bitters for a week (some soak it for as long as a month). This is then added to a batter of butter, sugar, molasses, and eggs. Baking for a few hours (and drizzling with a bit more cherry brandy) will result in a dark, rich dessert packed with flavor (and alcohol) that is a must-have on any table here on Christmas Day.

Formerly a British colony, Trinidad and Tobago adapted this dessert from traditional English fruitcakes and plum puddings. Every family has its own variation on the basic recipe and passes it from one generation to the next, so you can expect something different at any home you visit.

LES TREIZE DESSERTS:
A BAKER'S DOZEN OF DESSERTS

PROVENCE, FRANCE

*O*ne dessert is just not enough for those living in Provence. On December 24, Provence citizens enjoy the holiday feast they call *le gros souper* ("the big supper"), but they have to leave room for *les treize desserts de Noël*—the thirteen desserts of Christmas. These represent the twelve disciples plus Jesus, and though they are all sweet, the quantity is actually a bit more reasonable than "thirteen desserts" might initially sound.

All families include morsels from these eight categories:

- Walnuts or hazelnuts to symbolize the order of Saint Augustin.

- Raisins to symbolize the Dominican order.

- Dried figs to symbolize the Franciscan order.

- Almonds to symbolize the Carmelites. (Together, these first four desserts are known as *les mendicants*, or "the beggars," as the colors of the fruits are said to symbolize the colors of the monks' robes in the four original monastic communities of the Catholic Church.)

- An olive oil flatbread scented with orange blossoms, called a *fougasse* or *pompe à l'huile*. Whoever serves this bread must break it with their hands instead of cutting it to guarantee a good harvest in the New Year.

- A white nougat, made with hazelnuts and pine nuts, to symbolize good.

- A black nougat, made with almonds and caramelized honey, to symbolize evil.

- A plate of fresh fruit that includes oranges, pears, melons, plums, and grapes.

The other five dessert options can consist of dates stuffed with marzipan, dried plums, candied melon, thin waffles, and many others—this varies by region or by family, but the expectation is that at least twelve should be locally grown ingredients, while the thirteenth could be something more exotic. But in many homes, the children don't get to start eating sweets until they have named all the desserts.

The desserts would traditionally be served following midnight Mass, in simple bowls or plates set out on the dessert table. Today, those who go to the trouble of preparing *les treize desserts* are likely to provide something a bit more extravagant, stuffing the figs with chocolate rather than serving them plain, or presenting a fruit tart instead of a plate of simple fresh fruit. It seems when it comes to extravagant holiday celebrations, just offering thirteen desserts is not exciting enough.

PAVLOVA: A REFRESHING
CAKE INSPIRED BY A BALLERINA

AUSTRALIA AND NEW ZEALAND

*C*hristmas in this part of the world falls in the middle of summer, and celebrating the holiday on a beach or with a barbecue is not uncommon. Also essential to the festivities is serving pavlova, a meringue-encased cake with a gooey center, topped with whipped cream and colorful fruit (often kiwi, passionfruit, or strawberries).

It has been debated whether the recipe originated in Australia or New Zealand, but all agree that the name comes from the Russian ballerina Anna Pavlova, who visited the region during her world tour in 1926, when a hotel chef prepared the dessert for her, much to the dancer's delight. It held the moniker Pavlova ever since. While it is popular throughout the year in the region, it has become associated with the holidays, and can be shaped like a wreath to make it particularly Christmassy.

MULLED WINE:
THE PERFECT WINTER WARM-UP

NORTHERN EUROPE

*M*ot all sweet Christmas treats are eaten—plenty are imbibed. And if there is one drink synonymous with the holidays throughout northern Europe, it is mulled wine, a blend of booze, spices, and fruit that creates an intoxicating combination that warms one both inside and out. While there are some set standards to the drink, each country and culture has its own take and traditions around the beverage.

Scandinavian countries and Estonia enjoy the brightly colored *julglögg* or simply *glögg* (that's the Swedish spelling—in Denmark and Norway, it's *gløgg*) during the frigid Christmas season. Germany, Austria, and the Alsace region of France serve up *Glühwein*. Both terms translate as "glow," referring to the glowing heat applied to it. But it is also an appropriate term considering how the rum, vodka, or aquavit typically added to it can make one radiate. Red wine usually serves as the base, with a fair amount of sugar and spices such as cloves, cinnamon, ginger, vanilla, nutmeg, or star anise. Orange or lemon peels, chopped apples, raisins, or almonds might be added. It can be bought ready-made, complete with a picture of Santa on the bottle. But it is better to make one's own, which also allows the maker to tailor it to their preferred ingredients—and level of booziness.

SOURCES

Las Posadas: Festival of acceptance (Mexico)

"Las Posadas." *Encyclopedia Britannica online*. October 15, 2019.

Hickey, Conchita Cavazos. "Posadas, Las." *The Oxford Encyclopedia of Latinos and Latinas in the United States*. New York, NY: Oxford University Press, 2005. Oxford Reference.

Torres, T. "Posadas." *New Catholic Encyclopedia*, 2nd ed. Vol. 11. Toronto: Gale, 2003. 541-42.

Monyak, Suzanne. "For a Beautiful Religious Take on the Holiday Party, Consider *Las Posadas*." *Slate*. December 16, 2016.

Three Kings Day: Three cheers for the Magi (Spain and Latin America)

Iber, Jorge. "Tres Reyes." *The Oxford Encyclopedia of Latinos and Latinas in the United States*. New York, NY: Oxford University Press, 2005. Oxford Reference.

"Epiphany Celebrations Around the World." *New York Times*. January 6, 2018.

Denysenko, Nicholas E. *The Blessing of Waters and Epiphany: The Eastern Liturgical Tradition*. New York: Routledge, 2016.

Essick, Amber Inscone, and John Inscone Essick. "Distinctive Traditions of Epiphany." *Christmas and Epiphany*. Waco, TX: Baylor University, 2011. 69-74.

Pennick, Nigel. *Pagan Magic of the Northern Tradition: Customs, Rites, and Ceremonies*. Rochester, VT: Inner Traditions/Bear, 2015.

Derry, Johanna. "Let's Bring Back the Glorious Food Traditions of Twelfth Night (Largely, Lots of Cake)." *Telegraph*. January 4, 2016.

Muldoon, Molly. "Nollaig na mBan 2019—Women's Christmas Is Celebrated in Ireland Today." *IrishCentral*. January 6, 2019.

Sinterklaas Festival: The original holiday of gift giving (Netherlands and Belgium)

"St. Nicholas's Day." *Cultural Studies: Holidays Around the World*, 6th ed. Edited by Pearline Jaikumar. Detroit: Omnigraphics, 2018.

Gunn, Jeremy T. "Religious Symbols and Religious Expression in the Public Square." Davis, Derek H, ed. *The Oxford Handbook of Church and State in the United States*. New York: Oxford University Press, 2010. 276—310.

Weihnachtsmärkte: The bustling birthplace of modern Christmas (Germany)

Bowler, Gerry. "Germany." *The World Encyclopedia of Christmas*. Toronto: McClelland & Stewart, 2012.

Nissenbaum, Stephen. *The Battle for Christmas*. New York: Knopf Doubleday, 2010. 219-21.

Perry, Joe. *Christmas in Germany: A Cultural History*. Chapel Hill: University of North Carolina Press, 2010. 155-64.

"Christkindlesmarkt." *Cultural Studies: Holidays Around the World*, 6th ed. Edited by Pearline Jaikumar. Detroit: Omnigraphics, 2018.

Wilson, A. N. "'Tis the Season to Be JOLLY Grateful for Prince Albert!" *Mail on Sunday*. December 24, 2017. 14.

Saint Lucia Processions: Parade of white (Sweden)

"St. Lucy's Day." *Cultural Studies: Holidays Around the World*, 6th ed. Edited by Pearline Jaikumar. Detroit: Omnigraphics, 2018.

Tidholm, Po, and Agneta Lilja. *Celebrating the Swedish Way*. Swedish Institute. October 7, 2013. 43-45.

Crump, William D. "Sweden." *The Christmas Encyclopedia*, 3rd ed. Jefferson, NC: McFarland, 2013.

Haglund, Annica. "Golden-Haired Women Awaken Nobel Laureates on Lucia Day." *AP News*. December 12, 1990.

Burning the Devil: Cleansing evil spirits by bonfire (Guatemala)

Newman, Kate. "Burning the Devil in Guatemala." *National Geographic*. December 4, 2012.

Burnett, John. "Guatemalan Official: Burning Devil Dirties the Air." *NPR*. December 8, 2008.

Draven, James. "Antigua Guatemala: Volcanoes, Burning Devils, and a History of Resurrection." *Independent*. December 8, 2015.

Muldavin, Julia. "Burning the Old Year on the Beaches of Ecuador." *Meridian*. February 16, 2017.

Palmer, Alex. "Inside Scotland's Wild Ship-Building Viking Party." *Esquire*. February 7, 2017.

Nevins, Debbie, Falaq Kagda, and Magdalene Koh. *Hong Kong*. New York: Cavendish Square Publishing, 2017. 120.

"Broomsticks Burn in Spanish Festival." *Telegraph*. December 8, 2016.

Yule Log Night: Soaking up the year's bad luck (Latvia)

Barlas, Robert. *Latvia*. Singapore: Marshall Cavendish, 2000. 108.

"Latvian Christmas. Log Night in Old Riga." LiveRiga.com. October 16, 2019.

Bowler, Gerry. "Latvia." *The World Encyclopedia of Christmas*. Toronto: McClelland & Stewart, 2012.

Proclamation of Christmas Peace: Public call for order (Finland)

Christmas in Finland. Chicago: World Book, 2001. 22–24.

"The Declaration of Christmas Peace." Turku.fi.

Heinonen, Yrjö. "Cultural Memory of Sound and Space: The Case of the Declaration of Christmas Peace in Turku, Finland. *Memory, Space, Sound.* Ed. Johannes Brusila. Bristol, United Kingdom: Intellect, 2016.

il-Burbaba: Celebrating Saint Barbara (Jordon, Lebanon and Syria)

Gavlak, Dale. "In some countries, St. Barbara's Day helps kick off Christmas season." *Catholic News Service*. November 26, 2016.

"St. Barbara's Day." Cultural Studies: Holidays Around the World, 6th edition, edited by Pearline Jaikumar. Detroit, MI: Omnigraphics, Inc., 2018.

Kirtikar, Margo. *Once upon a Time in Baghdad.* Self-published: Xlibris Corporation, 2011. 272.

Crump, William D. "Israel." *The Christmas Encyclopedia*, 3rd ed. Jefferson, NC: McFarland, 2013.

Parrandas: A late-night musical strike (Puerto Rico)

Font-Guzman, J. *Experiencing Puerto Rican Citizenship and Cultural Nationalism*. New York, NY: Springer, 2016. 198.

Méndez-Méndez, Serafín, and Ronald Fernandez. *Puerto Rico Past and Present: An Encyclopedia*, 2nd ed. Santa Barbara, CA: ABC CLIO, 2015. 91.

Carols by Candlelight: Ensuring no one spends Christmas alone (Australia)

"Carols by Candlelight | History." *Only Melbourne.*

An Aussie Christmas. Perth, Australia: R.I.C. Publications, 2006. 59.

Gordon, Sharon. *Australia*. Singapore: Marshall Cavendish, 2005. 39.

Junkanoo: A Caribbean Christmas extravaganza (Bahamas)

"Junkanoo Festival." *Cultural Studies: Holidays Around the World*, 6th ed. Edited by Pearline Jaikumar. Detroit: Omnigraphics, 2018.

"Junkanoo Central." Educulture Bahamas.

"Bahamas." *Music in Latin America and the Caribbean: An Encyclopedic History,* Vol. 2, *Performing the Caribbean Experience.* Edited by Malena Kuss. Austin: University of Texas Press, 2007. 363.

Colinde: Ancient midwinter melodies (Romania and Moldova)

Ling, Jan. *A History of European Folk Music*. New York: University of Rochester Press, 1997. 68.

"Men's Group Colindat, Christmas-Time Ritual." Intangible Cultural Heritage, United Nations Educational, Scientific and Cultural Organization.

Zampogna: A Christmas bagpipe (Italy)

Lillie, Barry. "Zampognari Keep Alive the Tradition of Festive Bagpipe Playing." *Italy Magazine*, December 23, 2013.

Sullivan, Steve. "Pastorale di Natale (1917)—Pasquale Feis." *Encyclopedia of Great Popular Song Recordings.* Vol. 1. Lanham, MD: Scarecrow Press, 2013. 354.

Shooting In Christmas: Taking aim at evil spirits in the sky (Berchtesgaden, Germany)

"Christmas Shooting." *Cultural Studies: Holidays Around the World*, 6th ed. Edited by Pearline Jaikumar. Detroit: Omnigraphics, 2018.

"Christmas & New Year's Eve Shooters." Berchtesgaden.de.

Collins, Stella Ross. *Christmas!: Traditions, Celebrations and Food Across Europe.* London: Kyle Cathie, 1999. 12.

Parang Music: Singing Spanish once a year (Trinidad and Tobago)

Otis, John. "Trinidad and Tobago Remixes Caribbean Christmas Traditions." *NPR.* December 24, 2018.

Toussaint, Michael, et al. *Historical Dictionary of Trinidad and Tobago*. New York: Rowman & Littlefield Publishers, 2018. 140.

Birth, Kevin K. *Bacchanalian Sentiments: Musical Experiences and Political Counterpoints in Trinidad*. Durham, NC: Duke University Press, 2008. 119–27.

Mummering: Slightly terrifying Christmas visitors (Newfoundland and Labrador, Canada)

Doyle, Sabrina. "The Evolving Identity of Newfoundland's Outport Jannies." *Canadian Geographic*. December 24, 2015.

Laskow, Sarah. "The Long-Banned Tradition of Mummering in Newfoundland Is Making a Comeback." *Atlas Obscura*. December 13, 2016.

"The Jannies Were Here..." Live Rural Newfoundland and Labrador. January 5, 2013.

Bartlett, Steve. "Mummers Song Turns 25." *Telegraph*. December 28, 2007.

La Guignolée: Trick-or-treat for charity (Québec, Canada)

Lewis, John Oliver. "Twelve Habitant Songs." *Canadian Magazine* 59 (1922): 198–99.

Brault, Gerard J. *The French-Canadian Heritage in New England*. Lebanon, NH: University Press of New England, 1986. 18.

Devil's Knell: Incessant strikes of the bell (Dewsbury, Yorkshire, England)

Simpson, Jacqueline, and Stephen Roud. *A Dictionary of English Folklore*. New York: Oxford University Press, 2000.

"The Devil's Knell." GoDewsbury. December 22, 2012.

Holiday Book Flood: A tsunami of literary gifts (Iceland)

Jones, Meghan. "Why Every Book Lover Should Steal Iceland's Christmas Tradition." *Reader's Digest*.

Teicher, Jordan G. "Literary Iceland Revels in Its Annual 'Christmas Book Flood.'" *NPR*. December 25, 2012.

Knútsdóttir, Hildur. "The Jólabókaflóð." *Reykjavik Grapevine*. December 14, 2009.

Goldsmith, Rosie. "Iceland: Where One in 10 People Will Publish a Book." *BBC News*. October 14, 2013.

Christmas Swim: An invigorating start to Christmas Day (Ireland)

Jordan, Ailbhe, and Aengus O'Hanlon. "Swimmers Plunge into the Cold Irish Sea on Christmas Day." *Irish Mirror*. December 25, 2018.

Thompson, Sylvia. "Christmas and New Year Swims Around Ireland's Coast." *Irish Times*. December 23, 2017.

Christmas Sauna: Heating up before church (Finland)

McKenna, Amy, ed. *Denmark, Finland, and Sweden*. New York: Britannica Educational Publishing, 2013. 99.

Niendorf, Mariya. "Into the Steam, into the Dream: The Finnish Sauna as a Rite of Passage." Master's thesis. Indiana University, 2000. 25.

Bumba Meu Boi: Bringing back the bull (Brazil)

Bowler, Gerry. "Brazil." *The World Encyclopedia of Christmas*. Toronto: McClelland & Stewart, 2012.

Gottheim, Vivian I. "Bumba-Meu-Boi, a Musical Play from Maranhão." *World of Music* 30, no. 2 (1988): 40–68. JSTOR.

Hollander, Malika. *Brazil: The Culture*. New York: Crabtree Publishing, 2002. 10–11.

Mari Lwyd: Creepy horse with a penchant for poetry (Wales)

Howell, David. "Mari Lwyd: Intangible Heritage and the Performing Arts." *Wales Arts Review*. January 30, 2014.

Bowler, Gerry. "Mari Lwyd" and "Hodening Horse." *The World Encyclopedia of Christmas*. Toronto: McClelland & Stewart, 2012.

Meier, Allison. "The Skeletal Welsh Horse You Must Beat in a Battle of Rhymes." *Hyperallergic*. December 19, 2016.

Hawkins, Paul. *Bad Santas: And Other Creepy Christmas Characters*. New York: Simon & Schuster, 2013. 129.

Tió de Nadal: The friendly poop log (Catalonia, Spain)

"Tió de Nadal." *Atlas Obscura*.

Morton, Ella. "Feeding the Poop Log: A Catalan Christmas Tradition." *Slate*. December 24, 2013.

Bausells, Marta. "Letter of Recommendation: Tió de Nadal." *New York Times Magazine*. December 20, 2018.

Ritschel, Chelsea. "Meet Tió de Nadal, Catalonia's Smiling Christmas Log That Defecates Presents." *Independent*. December 4, 2017.

Harris, Simon. *Going Native in Catalonia*. Arcata, CA: Summertime Publishing, 2012.

Hunting the Wren: Raise high the dead bird (Ireland and Isle of Man)

Moore, A. W. *Folklore of the Isle of Man*. London: D. Nutt, 1891. 102–140.

Lawrence, Elizabeth Atwood. *Hunting the Wren: Transformation of Bird to Symbol: A Study in Human-Animal Relationships*. Knoxville: University of Tennessee Press, 1997.

Caine, Howard. "Hunting the Wren." *BBC*. December 23, 2005.

Flanagan, Kevin. "'Day of the Wren' and the 'Wren Boys.'" Brehon Law Academy. December 26, 2017.

Festa dos Rapazes: Boys on parade (Portugal)

Dunlop, Fiona. *National Geographic Traveler Portugal*. Washington, DC: National Geographic Society, 2005. 18.

"Festa dos Rapazes." Visit Portugal, Turismo de Portugal.

WinterFest: A secular symphony of lights (Hong Kong)

Chen, Piera. *Lonely Planet Hong Kong*. New York, NY: Lonely Planet, 2017.

"Hong Kong WinterFest." *Cultural Studies: Holidays Around the World*, 6th ed. Edited by Pearline Jaikumar. Detroit: Omnigraphics, 2018.

"Hong Kong WinterFest." Discover Hong Kong, Hong Kong Tourism Board.

Golden Pig: A hallucination promising good fortune (Czech Republic)

Ormsby, Eric. "Waiting for the Golden Pig." *New Criterion* 22, no. 6 (Feb. 2004): 43–47. EBSCOhost.

Laskow, Sarah. "Golden Pigs, Jesus-Shaped Bread, and 5 Other Delightful European Christmas Customs." *Atlas Obscura*. December 21, 2015.

Saint Nicholas/Sinterklaas (Netherlands and Belgium)

"Nicholas, St." *The Oxford Dictionary of the Christian Church*. Edited by F. L. Cross and E. A. Livingstone. Oxford University Press, 2009. Oxford Reference.

"Who Travels with St. Nicholas?" St. Nicholas Center.

Pimlott, John Alfred Ralph. *An Englishman's Christmas: A Social History*. Hassocks, UK: The Harvester Press, 1978. 85.

Bowler, Gerry. "Father Christmas." *The World Encyclopedia of Christmas*. Toronto: McClelland & Stewart, 2012.

Ciolli, Chris. "Stranger Than Santa: Europe's Most Unusual Christmas Characters." *AFAR*. November 23, 2015.

Joulupukki (Finland)

Harris, Kathleen. "How Joulupukki, the Finnish Santa, Went from Naughty to Nice." *Ink Tank.* December 22, 2015.

Raedisch, Linda. *The Old Magic of Christmas: Yuletide Traditions for the Darkest Days of the Year.* Woodbury, MN: Llewellyn Worldwide, 2013.

Nordland, Rod. "Santa in Finland, Where Marketing Triumphs Over Geography." *New York Times.* December 20, 2017.

Ded Moroz and Snegurochka: The grandfather-granddaughter holiday duo (Russia and Eastern Europe)

Dixon-Kennedy, Mike. *Encyclopedia of Russian & Slavic Myth and Legend.* Santa Barbara, CA: ABC-CLIO, 1998. 64.

Christmas in Russia. Chicago, IL: World Book, 2001.

"Veliky Ustyug—Hometown of Ded Moroz." Vologda Oblast Official Website.

Bowler, Gerry. *Christmas in the Crosshairs.* New York: Oxford University Press, 2017. 81–92.

Christkindl: Gift-bearing baby (Germany)

Sandford, John. *Encyclopedia of Contemporary German Culture.* Abingdon, UK: Taylor & Francis, 2013.

Steves, Rick. "Celebrating with the Christkind: A Germanic Christmas." Rick Steves' Europe.

Woodard, Joe. "The Enduring Power of Saint Nicholas." *Alberta Report.* 23, no. 1 (December 1995): 34.

Matt, Michael J. "An Advent Reflection: Waiting for the Christ Child." *The Remnant.* December 15, 2005.

Olentzero: Generous mountain giant (Basque)

Shults, Sylvia. *Spirits of Christmas: The Dark Side of the Holidays.* Hertford, NC: Crossroad Press, 2017.

Gall, Timothy L. *Worldmark Encyclopedia of Cultures and Daily Life*, 3rd ed. Vol. 5, *Europe.* Farmington Hills, MI: Gale, 2009. 61.

Hoteiosho: An all-seeing priest (Japan)

Crump, William D. "Japan." *The Christmas Encyclopedia*, 3rd ed. Jefferson, NC: McFarland, 2013.

Frau Holle: Well-dwelling witch (Germany)

Stern, James, et al. "Frau Holle." *The Complete Grimm's Fairy Tales*. London: Pantheon Books, 1972. 134–36.

"Holda." *The Hutchinson Unabridged Encyclopedia with Atlas and Weather Guide*. Abington, UK: Helicon, 2008.

Zipes, Jack. "Mother Holle." *The Oxford Companion to Fairy Tales*. Oxford, UK: Oxford University Press, 2005

La Befana: The benevolent Christmas witch (Italy)

"Befana Festival." *Cultural Studies: Holidays Around the World*, 6th ed. Edited by Pearline Jaikumar. Detroit: Omnigraphics, 2018.

Angelos, James. "The Season of the Witch: Forest Hills." *New York Times*. January 11, 2009.

Krampus: The Christmas devil (Austria)

Ridenour, Al. *The Krampus and the Old, Dark Christmas: Roots and Rebirth of the Folkloric Devil*. Port Townsend, WA: Feral House, 2016.

Ridenour, Al. "The Truth About Krampus." *Atlas Obscura*. November 29, 2013.

Billock, Jennifer. "The Origin of Krampus, Europe's Evil Twist on Santa." *Smithsonian* online. December 4, 2015.

Lauer-Williams, Kathy. "The History of Belsnickel: Santa's Cranky Cousin." *Morning Call*. November 29, 2013.

Christmas in France. Chicago: World Book, 1996. 16.

Cellania, Miss. "8 Legendary Monsters of Christmas." *Mental Floss*. December 21, 2017.

The Yule Lads and Grýla: A rowdy crew of mountain-dwelling pranksters (Iceland)

"First Yule Lads Arrive." *Iceland Review*. December 15, 2014.

Nuwer, Rachel. "Meet the Thirteen Yule Lads, Iceland's Own Mischievous Santa Clauses." *Smithsonian* online. December 17, 2013.

Palmer, Alex. "Why Iceland's Christmas Witch Is Much Cooler (and Scarier) Than Krampus." *Smithsonian* online. December 20, 2017.

Miles, Clement A. *Christmas in Ritual and Tradition*. London, UK: T. Fisher Unwin, 1912.

Kallikantzaroi: **Tree-chopping Christmas goblins (Greece, Bulgaria, and Serbia)**

Baker, Margaret. *Discovering Christmas Customs and Folklore: A Guide to Seasonal Rites*. London: Shire Publications, 2007. 108.

Raedisch, Linda. *The Old Magic of Christmas: Yuletide Traditions for the Darkest Days of the Year*. Woodbury, MN: Llewellyn Worldwide, 2013.

Buttnmandl: **Friendly neighborhood Riddle-Raddle Men (Berchtesgaden, Germany)**

Christmas in Today's Germany. Chicago: World Book, 1993. 34.

Ridenour, Al. *The Krampus and the Old, Dark Christmas: Roots and Rebirth of the Folkloric Devil*. Port Townsend, WA: Feral House, 2016.

Raedisch, Linda. *The Old Magic of Christmas: Yuletide Traditions for the Darkest Days of the Year.* Woodbury, MN: Llewellyn Worldwide, 2013.

Dancing Devils: Rambunctious holiday gift takers (Liberia)

Jarrett, Max Bankole. "Liberia's Dancing Christmas Devils Could Give Krampus a Lesson in Niceness." Goats and Soda, *NPR*. December 23, 2015.

Nyanseor, Siahyonkron. "The Origin of Liberian Santa Claus and Old Man Beggar." *Djogbachiachuwa: The Liberian Anthology*. Edited by Syrulwa Somah. Self-published, Xlibris US, 2012. 97.

"Celebrating Christmas in Liberia." *Douglas Review*. December 22, 2016.

Zwarte Piet: Sinterklaas's controversial companion (Netherlands)

Dechant, Dell. *The Sacred Santa: Religious Dimensions of Consumer Culture*. Eugene, OR: Wipf & Stock Publishers, 2008. 187–88.

Mackey, Robert. "A New Holiday Tradition for the Dutch: Arguing About Blackface." *New York Times*. November 14, 2014.

Bowler, Gerry. *Christmas in the Crosshairs*. New York: Oxford University Press, 2017. 159–60.

Waterfield, Bruno. "Dutch Father Christmas's Blacked-Up Helpers Banned for Being 'Racist.'" *Telegraph*. December 23, 2011.

Kassam, Ashifa. "Madrid Ends Blacking Up of Characters in Post-Christmas Tradition." *Guardian*. September 17, 2015.

Nativity Scenes: Creative cribs (Europe)

Anderson, L. V. "Who Staged the First Nativity Scene?" *Slate*. December 12, 2013.

Manning, Kathleen. "Who Invented the Nativity Scene?" *U.S. Catholic* 77, no. 12 (December 2012): 46.

"Probošt's Mechanical Christmas Crib." Museum of Nativity Scenes in Třebechovice, betlem.cz.

"Krýzovy jesličky." Muzeum Jindřichohradecka.

Adamek, Anna. "Cracovie ville belle et merveilleuse; Krakovian Szopka: From the Collection of the Historical Museum of the City of Krakow; Krakows Julkrubbor." *Material Culture Review/Revue de la culture matérielle* 46, no 1, 1997.

"Nativity Scene (Szopka) Tradition in Krakow." Intangible Cultural Heritage, United Nations Educational, Scientific and Cultural Organization. 2018.

Alech, Alice. "Noël Provençal." *Commonweal* 136, no. 22 (2009): 30.

Yule Goat: A combustible character (Sweden)

Raedisch, Linda. *The Old Magic of Christmas: Yuletide Traditions for the Darkest Days of the Year*. Woodbury, MN: Llewellyn Worldwide, 2013.

O'Leary, Margaret Hayford. *Culture and Customs of Norway*. Santa Barbara, CA: ABC-CLIO, 2010.

"About the Gävle Goat." Visit Gävle.

John, J. *A Christmas Compendium*. London: Continuum International Publishing, 2005. 67.

Paról: Lanterns light the way (Philippines)

"Philippines." *Junior Worldmark Encyclopedia of World Holidays*. Vol. 1. Edited by Robert H. Griffin and Ann H. Shurgin. Farmington Hills, MI: UXL, 2000. 103–9.

Lopez, Mellie Leandicho. *A Handbook of Philippine Folklore*. Quezon City, PH: University of the Philippines Press, 2006. 355.

"Giant Lantern Festival." City of San Fernando.

Pōhutukawa: Kiwi Christmas tree (New Zealand)

Katz, Brigit. "New Zealand's Iconic Pōhutukawa Tree May Have Roots in Australia." *Smithsonian* online. June 23, 2017.

Low, Tim. "Australia's Giant Parasitic Christmas Tree." *Australian Geographic*. May 15, 2017.

Himmeli: Merry mobiles (Finland)

Perry, Nicole. "Himmeli for the Holidays: How to Make These Chic and Structured Ornaments and Wreath." *CBC Life*. December 22, 2017.

Basinger, Rachel. "How to Make a Himmeli Sculpture." *Guardian*. June 6, 2014.

Pavuchky: Celebratory spiderwebs (Ukraine)

Vaughn, Mary Ann Woloch. *Ukrainian Christmas: Traditions, Folk Customs, and Recipes*. Munster, IN: Ukranian Heritage Company, 1983.

Tracz, Orysia Paszczak. "A Spider for Christmas?" *Ukrainian Weekly* 74, no. 53 (December 31, 2006).

Katchanovski, Ivan, Zenon E. Kohut, Bohdan Y. Nebesio, and Myroslav Yurkevich. *Historical Dictionary of Ukraine*. Lanham, MD: Scarecrow Press, 2013. 180–81.

Dziad and Baba: A chandelier of wheat (Poland)

Knab, Sophie Hodorowicz. *Polish Customs, Traditions and Folklore*. New York: Hippocrene Books, 1993. 33.

Polanie Club, Inc. *Treasured Polish Christmas Customs and Traditions*. Minneapolis: Polanie Publishing, 1972. 122–23.

Kmiec, Stas. "Polish Christmas Ornaments." *Polish American Journal*. December 2006.

Chichilaki: A shaggy Christmas tree (Georgia)

"Celebrating Christmas in Georgia—The Holiday Which Unites the Entire Country." *Georgian Journal*. January 5, 2018.

"Georgians Rediscover Christmas Tree Traditions." *BBC*. December 21, 2011.

Bardzimashvili, Temo. "Georgia Kicks Off New Year with Post-Modern Christmas Tree." *Eurasianet*. December 22, 2009. Archived.

Spilling, Michael, Winnie Wong, and Debbie Nevins. *Georgia*. New York: Cavendish Square Publishing, 2017. 118.

"Alilo—Christmas Tradition in Georgia." *Georgian Journal*. January 8, 2019.

Marshall, Dan. "Blessing of the Badnjak." *World & I* 16, no. 1 (January 2001): 172. EBSCOhost.

Badnjak: A complex Christmas log (Croatia and Serbia)

Miles, Clement A. "The Yule Log." *Christmas in Ritual and Tradition*. London: T. Fisher Unwin, 1912.

Spicer, Dorothy Gladys. *Folk Festivals and the Foreign Community*. Farmington Hills, MI: Gale Research Company, 1976. 144–45.

Rihtman-Auguštin, Dunja. *Christmas in Croatia*. Zagreb, Croatia: Golden Marketing, 1997. 59–60.

Night of the Radishes: Elaborate sculptures made of root vegetables (Oaxaca, Mexico)

Godoy, Maria. "Survived the Mayan Apocalypse? Here Come the Radish People." The Salt, *NPR*. December 22, 2012.

Lowry, Tara. "Radiant Radishes: La Noche de Rabanos in Oaxaca." *Mexconnect*. December 22, 2012.

Sinterklaasgedicht: Roasting the ones you love with poetry (Netherlands)

Seward, Pat, et al. *Netherlands*. New York: Cavendish Square, 2016. 116.

Maas, Monica. "Dutch Sinterklaas 'Surprises.'" St. Nicholas Center.

Faber, Paul, and Philippa Burton. *Sinterklaas Overseas: The Adventures of a Globetrotting Saint*. Amsterdam: KIT Publishers, 2006.

Holy Innocents' Day Pranks: April Fools in December (Spain, Philippines, and Latin America)

Alejandro, Reynaldo G., and Marla Yotoko Chorengel. *Pasko! The Philippine Christmas*. Manila, Philippines: National Book Store, 1998.

Phillips, Jennifer. *In the Know in Mexico & Central America: The Indispensable Guide to Working and Living in Mexico & Central America*. Telford, PA: Diversified Publishing, 2003.

Sierra, Lisa, and Tony Sierra. "How Spain Celebrates the Holy Innocents Day." The Spruce Eats. August 12, 2019.

Ganna: Holiday hockey (Ethiopia)

Knox, Jules. "An Ethiopian Christmas." *Star*. January 6, 2012.

Bowler, Gerry. "Ethiopia." *The World Encyclopedia of Christmas*. Toronto: McClelland & Stewart, 2012.

Alamayahu, Samuel. "The Game of Ganna." *University College Ethnological Society Bulletin, Addis Ababa* 9 (1959): 9–27.

Survakane: A lucky Christmas swat (Bulgaria)

"Christmas Traditions in Bulgaria." Eufriend. 2005.

"Traditions, Crafts, and Ethnography: Survaknitsa." Bulgarian Ministry of Economy, Energy, and Tourism.

Aguinaldos: Holiday battle for points (Colombia)

Pedraza, Marta. "*¿Pajita en boca? ¿Beso robado? Conoce los 5 mejores aguinaldos para jugar con tu pareja,*" *Zank You.* December 12, 2018.

"How Colombians Celebrate Christmas," *Impulse Travel.* December 10, 2018.

Lotería de Navidad: Very generous Christmas present (Spain)

"What Is El Gordo, the Annual Christmas Lottery Called the 'Fat One' in Spain?" *Telegraph.* December 22, 2016.

Hodge, Mark. "'The Fat One': What Is El Gordo, What Does It Mean and How Much Can You Win in the 2018 Spanish Christmas Lottery?" *Sun.* November 12, 2018.

Christmas in Spain. Chicago, IL: World Book, Incorporated, 1996. 25.

Christmas Crackers: Explosive treats (England)

McAlpine, Fraser. "A Very British Christmas Part 3: Crackers." *BBC America.* December 2011.

Forsyth, Mark. *A Christmas Cornucopia: The Hidden Stories Behind Our Yuletide Traditions.* London: Penguin UK, 2016. 165.

Arikoglu, Lale. "Airlines Ban Christmas Crackers, to the Dismay of British Travelers." *Conde Nast Traveler.* November 27, 2017.

"Largest Christmas Cracker." *Guinness World Records.*

Twelve-Dish Supper: A meat-free feast (Eastern and Central Europe)

Kasprzyk-Chevriaux, Magdalena. "The 12 Dishes of Polish Christmas." Culture.pl. December 12, 2013.

Yakovenko, Svitlana. *Ukrainian Christmas Eve Supper: Traditional Village Recipes for Sviata Vecheria.* Lidcombe, AUS: Sova Books, 2016.

Goldstein, Darra, et al. *Culinary Cultures of Europe: Identity, Diversity and Dialogue.* Council of Europe, 2005. 269.

Helbig, Adriana, Oksana Buranbaeva, and Vanja Mladineo. *Culture and Customs of Ukraine.* Santa Barbara, CA: ABC-CLIO, 2008. 113.

Lechón de Nochebuena: A whole hog for the holidays (Spain, Philippines, and Latin America)

Cordle, Ina Paiva. "On Nochebuena, Many in South Florida Will Be Roasting a Pig in a 'Caja China.'" *Miami Herald*. December 23, 2013.

"A Puerto Rican Christmas." *El Boricua*.

Manahan, Millie. "Manila or Cebu Lechon: A Staple Filipino Food for All Occasions." *When in Manila*. July 13, 2017.

Lutefisk: An offensively delightful Christmas fish (Norway and the Midwestern United States)

Johnson, Steve. "Ah! Lutefisk." *Chicago Tribune*. December 11, 1989.

O'Leary, Margaret Hayford. *Culture and Customs of Norway*. Santa Barbara, CA: ABC-CLIO, 2010. 81–83.

Janik, Erica. "Scandinavians' Strange Holiday Lutefisk Tradition." *Smithsonian* online. December 8, 2011.

Tourtière: Meat pie for the holidays (Québec, Canada)

Lusted, Marica Amidon. "Eat Like a Canadian." *Faces* 35, no. 8 (May 2019): 26. EBSCOhost.

Bramen, Lisa. "Tourtière: Québecois for Christmas." *Smithsonian* online. December 7, 2011.

Hallacas: Stuffed cornmeal turnovers (Venezuela)

Maddicks, Russell. *Venezuela—Culture Smart! The Essential Guide to Customs & Culture*. London: Kuperard, 2012.

Padgett, Tim. "A Yuletide Treat Recalls Venezuela's Christmas Past." *America* 217, no. 14 (December 2017): 15. EBSCOhost.

Il Capitone: Fried eel festivities (Southern Italy)

Lord, Christine. "Splendors and Surprises of a Christmas Abroad." *New York Times*. December 24, 1978.

Ross, Corine. *Christmas in Italy*. Chicago: World Book, 1990. 58.

Claiborne, Craig. "A Seven-Course Feast of Fish." *New York Times*. December 16, 1987.

Clark, Melissa. "Surf's Up on Christmas Eve." *New York Times*. December 18, 2013.

Forty-Three-Day Fast: A month and a half without meat (Egypt)

Fieldhouse, Paul. "Coptic Feasts and Fasts." *Food, Feasts, and Faith: An Encyclopedia of Food Culture in World Religions.* Vol. 1. Santa Barbara, CA: ABC-CLIO, 2017. 135–39.

Morgan, Robert. *History of the Coptic Orthodox People and the Church of Egypt.* Victoria, BC: FriesenPress, 2016. 235–36.

Dopp i Gryta: A fondue to remember famine (Sweden)

Barber, Elizabeth Wayland. "God Jul! Swedish Midwinter Customs—Then and Now." *Folk Dance Scene* 52 no. 10 (December 2016): 4–6. EBSCOhost.

Williams, Jasmin K. "A Swedish Christmas." *New York Post.* December 12, 2007.

Marbinda: Sharing the cow (North Sumatra, Indonesia)

Crump, William D. "Indonesia." *The Christmas Encyclopedia,* 3rd ed. Jefferson, NC: McFarland, 2013. 404.

Olsson, Nils William. "Christmas As Celebrated in My Childhood." *Swedish American Genealogist* 25, no. 4 (December 2005): 1–3. EBSCOhost.

Weissgerber, Hans. *The Church and the Confessions: The Role of the Confessions in the Life and Doctrine of the Lutheran Churches.* Minneapolis: Fortress Press, 1963. 130.

"Unique Traditions of Christmas Celebration in Indonesia." Sun Education Group. November 14, 2017.

Jollof Rice: A one-pot staple (West Africa)

LeVert, Suzanne. *Cultures of the World: Sierra Leone.* Singapore: Marshall Cavendish, 2007. 118.

Oderinde, Busayo. "The Nigerian Versus Ghanaian Jollof Rice Debate." BellaNaija. July 5, 2015.

"A Regal Holiday Dinner: West African Jollof." *New York Amsterdam News* 93, no. 50 (December 12, 2002): 28. EBSCOhost.

Little Feast: Breaking a long fast (Iran)

Wernecke, Herbert H. *Celebrating Christmas Around the World.* Louisville, KY: Westminster Press, 1999. 67.

Kentucky for Christmas: A fitting feast for a Western celebration (Japan)

Chandler, Adam. *Drive-Thru Dreams: A Journey Through the Heart of America's Fast-Food Kingdom*. New York: Flatiron Books, 2019.

Smith, K. Annabelle. "Why Japan Is Obsessed with Kentucky Fried Chicken on Christmas." *Smithsonian* online. December 14, 2012.

Barton, Eric. "Why Japan Celebrates Christmas with KFC." *BBC Worklife*. December 19, 2016.

Osawa, Juro. "Japanese Dream of a Romantic Christmas." *Wall Street Journal*. December 20, 2012.

Roscón de Reyes: A dessert hiding a secret prize (Spain)

Miranda, Maria T. "The Feast of *Los Reyes Magos*." *Encyclopedia of Latino Culture: From Calaveras to Quinceañeras*. Edited by Charles M. Tatum. Santa Barbara: ABC-CLIO, 2013. 274–75.

Lebovitz, David. "Galette des rois." Davidlebovitz.com. January 5, 2014.

Hatic, Dana. "The King Cake Tradition, Explained." *Eater*. January 4, 2018.

Papadopoulos, Madina. "A Short History of King Cake's Long History." *Paste*. February 5, 2016.

Dennison's Christmas Book: Suggestions for Christmas, New Years and Twelfth Night Parties. Framingham, MA: Dennison Manufacturing Company, 1923. 26.

MacClain, Alexia. "Twelfth Night Traditions: A Cake, a Bean, and a King." *Unbound, Smithsonian Libraries Blog*. January 4, 2013.

Oplatek: Breaking the wafer (Poland)

Zielinski, Sarah. "Polish Christmas Wafer: A Flavorless Tradition That's Oh So Sweet." The Salt, *NPR*. December 24, 2012.

Knab, Sophie Hodorowicz. *Polish Customs, Traditions and Folklore*. New York: Hippocrene Books, 1993. 36–40.

Plachta, Louise. "Platcha: A Traditional Polish Christmas." *Oakland Press*. December 22, 2017.

Apples: A healthy holiday gift (China)

O'Donnell, Bridget. "Explainer: Why China Celebrates Christmas with Apples." *That's Mag*. December 24, 2018.

Makinen, Julie. "In China, Nothing Says Merry Christmas Like...an Apple?" *Los Angeles Times*. December 26, 2013.

Kuo, Lily. "Chinese Cities Crack Down on Christmas Celebrations." *Guardian*. December 24, 2018.

Risalamande: Holiday rice pudding (Denmark)

Pedersen, Anne. "It's Risengrød! Danish Rice Porridge." Smithsonian Center for Folklife & Cultural Heritage. December 22, 2014.

"Legend of the Nisse and Tomte." Ingebretsen's Nordic Marketplace.

Scott, Astrid Karlsen. "A Norwegian Christmas." *World & I* 10, no. 12 (December 1995): 132. EBSCOhost.

Marzipan Pig: Sweet swine (Norway and Germany)

Woolsey, Barbara. "Marzipan Pigs Are the Sweetest Way to Celebrate New Year's in Germany." *Vice Munchies*. December 24, 2015.

Noah's Pudding: The oldest dessert in the world (Armenia)

Arsiya, Izlem. "The Oldest Dessert in the World: Ashura" *Daily Sabah*. March 11, 2014.

"Anoush Abour or Noah's Pudding." *Dining in Diaspora*. January 1, 2018.

"Noah's Pudding." Community Dialogue Manual Series. London: Dialogue Society, 2011.

Kulkuls: Sweet coconut curls (India)

Peters-Jones, Michelle. "How We Celebrate Christmas in India." *Kitchn*. December 16, 2014.

Randhap, Ruchik. "Kidyo/Kidiyo/Kulkuls (Sweet Dough Curls)." *Ruchik Randhap: Food & Memories of Mangalore*. December 2, 2011.

Bûche de Noël: A Yule log made to be eaten (France)

Riely, Elizabeth Gawthrop. "Bûche de Noël." *The Oxford Companion to Sugar and Sweets*. Edited by Darra Goldstein. New York: Oxford University Press, 2015. Oxford Reference.

Butler, Stephanie. "The Delicious History of the Yule Log." History.com. December 21, 2012.

Waldee, Lynne Marie. *Cooking the French Way*. New York, NY: Lerner Publishing, 2009. 66.

Szaloncukor: A decoration and a treat, all in one (Hungary)

Gyori, Robert. "Szaloncukor, the Hungarian Christmas Candy."
VisitBudapest.travel. December 13, 2010.

Cozonac: Holiday Christmas bread (Romania and Moldova)

Rolek, Barbara. "Cozonac: Romanian Easter and Christmas Bread."
The Spruce Eats. November 10, 2019.

Black Fruitcake: A boozy, time-intensive treat (Trinidad and Tobago)

"How to Make Trinidad's Famous Black Cake." *Caribbean Journal*. December
3, 2016.

Les Treize Desserts: A baker's dozen of desserts (Provence, France)

Millo, François, and Viktorija Todorovska. *Provence Food and Wine: The Art
of Living*. Evanston, IL: Agate Publishing, 2014. 65.

Pavlova: A refreshing cake inspired by a ballerina (Australia and New Zealand)

Brennan, Georgeanne. *La Vie Rustic: Cooking and Living in the French
Style*. Sydney: Weldon Owen, 2017. 126.

Leach, Helen. *The Pavlova Story: A Slice of New Zealand's Culinary History*.
Dunedin, NZ: Otago University Press, 2008.

Mulled Wine: The perfect winter warm-up (Northern Europe)

Gabay, Elizabeth. "Mulled Wine." *The Oxford Companion to Sugar and
Sweets*. Edited by Darra Goldstein. New York, NY: Oxford University
Press, 2015. Oxford Reference.

INDEX

ALEX PALMER is a journalist who covers business, travel, and pop culture for publications like the *New York Post, Time Out New York, Billboard,* and Huffington Post. He is the author of *Weird-o-pedia: The Ultimate Collection of Surprising, Strange, and Incredibly Bizarre Facts About (Supposedly) Ordinary Things* and *Literary Miscellany: Everything You Always Wanted to Know About Literature.*